Rottweilers

TAMMY GAGNE

Rottweiler

Project Team
Editor: Stephanie Fornino
Copy Editor: Joann Woy
Interior Design: Leah Lococo Ltd. and Stephanie Krautheim
Design Layout: Patricia Escabi

T.F.H. Publications
President/CEO: Glen S. Axelrod
Executive Vice President: Mark E. Johnson
Publisher: Christopher T. Reggio
Production Manager: Kathy Bontz

T.F.H. Publications, Inc.
One TFH Plaza
Third and Union Avenues
Neptune City, NJ 07753

Discovery Communications, Inc. Book Development Team
Maureen Smith, Executive Vice President & General
    Manager, Animal Planet
Carol LeBlanc, Vice President, Licensing
Elizabeth Bakacs, Vice President, Creative Services
Peggy Ang, Director, Animal Planet Marketing
Caitlin Erb, Licensing Specialist

Printed and bound in China
07 08 09 10 11 1 3 5 7 9 8 6 4 2

Library of Congress Cataloging-in-Publication Data
Gagne, Tammy.
Rottweilers / Tammy Gagne.
p. cm. – (Animal planet pet care library)
Includes index.
ISBN-13: 978-0-7938-3775-5 (alk. paper)
1. Rottweiler dog. I. Title.
SF429.R7G34 2007
636.73–dc22
2006030265

The Leader In Responsible Animal Care For Over 50 Years!™
www.tfh.com

Table of **Contents**

Chapter 1

Why I Adore My

Rottweiler

Many of the most admirable human traits can be found in a Rottweiler. Loyalty, strength, and a great zest for life are all part of this remarkable breed's nature. When treated with love and respect, this is a dog capable of surpassing many humans in his ability to strike that elusive balance of shrewd intelligence and unconditional love—a feat that perhaps only a dog can truly manage.

In addition to being smart, Rottweilers can be extremely playful, which makes training an easy and enjoyable task. Sadly, training often means first undoing damage that a previous owner has perpetrated. Like the Rottweiler breed itself, responsible owners must strike a balance between empowering their dogs with love and making sure that they understand their place in the family and in society. Unlike a Golden Retriever or a Beagle, you see, the Rottweiler is expected to be both intrepid and humble in the face of his many friends and foes. Fortunately, most Rottweilers appear to enjoy a challenge and revel in the praise for a job well done.

Whether you have loved Rottweilers for many years or they are completely new to you, you will likely feel compelled to take a second look at this beautiful animal whenever you see one. As an American Kennel Club (AKC) judge put it to me recently, the breed's majestic color combination can make the dog look like a small horse. Of course, the Rottweiler's beauty goes much further

than skin deep, but like a handsome Hollywood movie star, it is difficult to describe the dog's unique appeal without acknowledging this more superficial reason to fancy the breed.

A Working History

Theories about the Rottweiler's origins are numerous. Many believe that the breed descended from a mastiff-type drover dog whom the Romans used when they conquered Europe. Some insist that the breed is entirely German, originating from the town of Rottweil—hence the breed's modern name. These fanciers assert that the breed was developed by native butchers, who then dubbed the breed Rottweiler Metzgerhund (butcher dog). Still others claim that the Rottweiler descended from the Bouvier.

No matter which history you deem the correct one (or whether you think that all may have some veracity), one common thread exists—the breed's long-lived penchant for working. The Romans were believed to have used Rottweilers to herd the sheep and cattle that fed their armies. The Germans were also said to have used the dogs for herding their cattle to market and as beasts of burden for carrying things. During war times throughout history,

Rottweilers

Loyalty, strength, and a great zest for life are all part of the Rottweiler's nature.

Seeing Stars

Famous Rottweiler owners include actress Alicia Silverstone, Everclear bass guitar player Craig Montoya, and comedian Jay Mohr. Actors and real-life husband and wife Will Smith and Jada Pinkett Smith own four Rottweilers. Jada credits their canine crew and their regular walking sessions for helping her stay in shape.

Rottweilers have been utilized over and over again as guard dogs.

Today's Rottweilers have discovered a whole new world of activities open to them. While many still work as guard dogs, others have found their niche as police dogs or registered therapy dogs. Many Rottweilers also enjoy competitive events such as conformation, agility, and obedience trials.

A member of the Working Group, the Rottweiler is one of the most versatile dogs in existence. He is at once strong and gentle, intelligent but not resistant to training, and hardworking, yet unabashedly playful when it's time for fun. In addition to all this, he has the look of an old soul that makes so many people feel instantly at ease when in his presence.

A Sight to Behold

The overall look of the Rottweiler exudes strength and durability. Size and stature certainly play a supporting role in his robust appearance, but correct proportion is also essential. One might say that Rottweilers are built like marathon runners—made for endurance as opposed to speed.

Size

Although the AKC standard states that male dogs should stand between 24 and 27 inches (61.0 and 68.6 cm) tall and females should measure 22 to 25 inches (55.8 to 63.5 cm), in both cases the mid-range of this designation is preferred for conformation. Again, though, proportion is more important than exact measurement, as long as the dog meets the general requirements for size.

Coat

The Rottweiler's outer coat is straight, coarse, and dense. Of medium length, it lies flat against the body. An undercoat should be present on the neck and thighs, but it should not show through the outer coat. The climate in which a dog lives may affect the amount of his undercoat. Shortest on the dog's head, ears, and legs, the outer coat is typically longest on the rump and hind legs.

Rottweilers are predominately black with rust or mahogany-colored markings.

Color

Rottweilers are predominantly black with striking rust or mahogany-colored markings. The boundaries for the two colors should be clearly defined, and the accent color should only appear over the eyes, on the side of the muzzle, and on the throat, chest, and lower legs. It is also present under the dog's tail. Any base color other than black is a disqualification, according to the AKC.

Head and Expression

The Rottweiler head is another distinctively broad feature. When viewed from the side, the forehead should be moderately arched. Ideally, the forehead should be smooth, although some wrinkling may occur when the dog is alert. A Rottweiler's expression should be one of dignity and self-assurance.

Eyes

The dog's almond-shaped eyes are of medium size, with well-fitting lids. They should neither protrude nor recede. The universal color is dark brown. Yellow eyes, also know as bird-of-prey eyes, are considered a serious fault according to the AKC, as are eyes of different colors or sizes or a hairless eye rim.

Ears

The medium-sized ears are triangular in shape and carried level with the top of the skull when the dog is alert. This gives the head an even wider appearance. Hanging forward with the inner edge lying close to the head, the ears should typically fall no lower than the middle of the dog's cheek. Ears protruding outward or ears that are creased or wrinkled are also classified as a serious fault according to the AKC.

Temperament and Personality

A Rottweiler's temperament will depend on many factors, such as breeding, environment, and the dog's history. However, by making love and kindhearted training regular parts of his life, you will bring out the best of your dog's unique nature.

Aggressiveness

If you own a Rottweiler, you have probably been asked many times about the breed's viciousness. In fact, in recent years, few breeds have encountered the same level of cynicism and distrust from society as the Rottweiler. The entire breed has been blamed for some horrific acts, some of which have brought deadly consequences to both humans and animals. National headlines sensationalizing these incidents have branded the breed with a scarlet letter of sorts, only unlike Nathaniel Hawthorne's infamous symbol, in the case of these stories, the "A" stands for aggression.

Is there such a thing as an aggressive dog? Of course. Aggression is a very serious problem that can rapidly spiral out of control with any canine breed when a dog is allowed to take over the alpha position within a household—or worse, if a dog is mistreated or trained to be a ruthless attack animal. Frequently, the result is an animal who trusts no one and who is also completely untrustworthy himself.

Although temperaments vary, most breeders recommend a female Rottweiler for first-time owners. Females are typically smaller than males and therefore easier to control. They are also known for being less dominant and generally more affectionate.

It is vital to understand that blaming the breed for the actions of a particular dog is both unfair and impractical. Classifying an entire breed as dangerous is as irresponsible as assuming that another breed is incapable of aggression. Every dog is different. When bred responsibly and properly care for by a devoted owner, the Rottweiler is among the very best canine companions.

Eagerness to Please

The Rottie (a term used by those fondest of the breed) is most concerned with pleasing his owner. Although many Rotties can be stubborn—or even clownlike at

The Expert Knows

The Rise of the Rottweiler

Although the first Rottweiler was admitted to the AKC studbook in 1931, the breed was fairly uncommon for nearly the next 50 years. This all changed in the early 1980s, though, when the breed's popularity began soaring. For nearly two decades now, the Rottweiler has ranked among the most registered breeds with the AKC.

times—this loyal breed is impressively focused. Your dog will usually be happiest when you are pleased with his performance. Unlike many other breeds that are overtaken by their urge to run after small animals, Rottweilers possess an impressive attention span and tend to stay close to their people instead of giving chase. Also, unlike many other breeds, they do not usually bark simply for the sake of making noise. If your Rottweiler is barking, there is usually a reason.

SENIOR DOG TIP

The Mature Rottweiler

Most dogs officially achieve senior-citizen status when they enter the final third of their lives. For the Rottweiler, this is typically between the ages of 6 and 8. Although many Rotties are surpassing their projected lifespan of between 9 and 12 years, most owners will likely begin seeing signs of aging well before this time. A senior dog's life can still be a full one, but he may need to rest a little more and play a little less intensely as he moves from adulthood into his senior years.

Friendliness

Although your Rottie will always want to meet your friends, he will most likely return to you as soon as he is done assessing their intentions. He may not warm up to strangers quickly, but once he offers his friendship, it will probably be for keeps. This is a dog with an excellent memory and a keen intuition. Treat him well, and he will be in service to you for a lifetime, but mistreat him, and he will never truly get past it.

Protectiveness

Although the Rottweiler does have some protective instincts, many other breeds are better suited to the role of guarding the family home. If you want a watchdog who will alert you to strangers approaching your house, consider a Labrador Retriever, a Standard Poodle, or even a terrier breed instead. Although they possess an innate desire to protect those they love, Rottweilers need extensive training before they can safely apply this natural instinct.

Trainability

You may have heard that certain breeds are more difficult to train than others. Fortunately, the Rottweiler is not one of these more challenging breeds, but like everything else about an individual animal, trainability can vary from dog to dog. In general, Rotties are highly intelligent. You can also help increase your dog's chances for success by starting the training process early. Whether you purchase a Rottweiler puppy or adopt an adult dog, your commitment to training will matter just as much as your dog's aptitude for learning.

Know that owning a Rottweiler comes with considerable responsibility. Your primary goal must be to make training a lifelong process. This can consume a substantial amount of your time, and it must never be an obligation that looms at the bottom of your to-do list, getting postponed in favor of seemingly more urgent tasks. Just as you must walk your dog regularly to properly housetrain him, you must also make sure that his behavior-related training is given sufficient priority. While housetraining accidents can easily be cleaned up and forgotten, one physical altercation could be catastrophic for both you and your dog.

This wondrous breed offers countless joys to their owners' lives. Their huge hearts are filled with an unlimited amount of love, and they expect so little in return. The impact of what we do give our pets, though, is invaluable to both our dogs and our relationships with them. Owning a Rottweiler demands great responsibility on an owner's behalf. Take that responsibility seriously, and

FAMILY-FRIENDLY TIP

How Are Rotties With Children?

A properly bred Rottweiler who receives adequate socialization and training will generally get along fine with children, but tolerance will vary from dog to dog. He must be taught early on what is acceptable behavior and what is not, as should the child. Because of their large size and inherent desire to herd, Rottweilers should always be supervised around children. A minor bump can cause serious injury to a small child. Also, some Rottweilers have a high degree of prey drive (the instinct to chase moving objects), and therefore, they should never be left alone with children, who naturally will want to run and play. Some breeders recommend waiting until the children are at least school age before introducing a Rottweiler into the home. The amount of space in your home, the age of your children, and the amount of time the dog will be in contact with the children should be part of your decision.

(Courtesy of the American Rottweiler Club)

you will end up with a steadfast companion worthy of all the time and effort you invest in him.

Chapter 2

The Stuff of

Everyday Life

As you get to know your Rottweiler, you will likely discover the things that he likes best, just as I have with my dogs. This is why I encourage new dog owners to pace themselves in filling their shopping baskets with all the enticing items that call to them from the store shelves. There will be plenty of time to determine which of these may be fun or useful to you and your new dog. In the meantime, there are several other items that nearly all new Rottweiler owners need.

A dog bed will provide your pet with a comfortable sleeping area.

Bed

It is tempting to allow that cute little Rottweiler puppy to sleep on the foot of your bed. After all, he doesn't take up that much space. As he grows larger, though, you will likely find this sleeping arrangement to be less than ideal, particularly if you have more than one dog. For this reason, you may want to provide your dog with a bed of his own. Some dogs prefer sleeping in their crates, and this is also a sensible choice. If your dog's crate is located too far from your bedroom, though, and you'd prefer that he sleep closer to you, a dog bed may be the answer.

Dog beds are available in a wide array of styles and fabrics. Perhaps you can imagine your Rottie curling up on a striking rust-colored round bolster design that matches his coat, or maybe he'd prefer a fleece-covered rectangular model stuffed with comfy orthopedic foam. Whatever model suits the two of you, be sure to select one that is spacious enough to accommodate your larger breed.

Although you will pay a relatively high price for a quality dog bed, this is one item that your Rottweiler should have for quite some time, so it is usually worth the investment. To ensure that you do not have to replace it within just weeks or months, I advise waiting until your dog is through with both teething and housetraining to make this purchase. Until this time, his crate or an old folded blanket will work just fine as an impromptu bed. No matter what your dog's age or housetraining reliability, choose a bed with a zip-off cover for easy cleaning, because it will inevitably need laundering from time to time. I have also found that beds with zipper access to the interior tend to last longer than those sewn shut, because their stuffing can be refilled if they become too flat from wear.

Collar

Similar to his leash, your dog's collar should be made of a strong yet comfortable material. Although leather is the most durable, you will likely have trouble finding a leather collar made with breakaway technology, a brilliant feature available on most nylon designs. This may be less of a concern if you remove your Rottweiler's collar when he isn't being walked, but it could literally save his life if a strangulation risk ever presents itself. My breeder won't even keep collars on any of her dogs when inside for fear of this happening.

A good alternative for many owners who find leash training to

A durable nylon collar is a good choice for your Rottie.

be an especially challenging task is a head-halter lead or a no-pull harness. Both these devices are currently made by several different companies that focus on humanely controlling your dog while walking him. They are praised for being extremely comfortable and never pinching or choking your animal. Even with this item, though, you may find it necessary to seek the input of a professional trainer. In this or any other training situation, never underestimate the value of professional advice.

I am not a fan of the pinch or prong-style choke collars (choke collars that literally push metal spikes into a dog's neck) because of their capacity for causing serious injury to a pet. If your dog is one who will continue pulling even while wearing a choke collar, he may be seriously wounded if affixed with one of these more extreme variations. If you are having trouble preventing your Rottweiler from pulling you off your feet, you are not alone. Many Rottie owners have faced this common problem, but the answer is training him, not hurting him.

Setting a Schedule

The best time to incorporate a schedule into your Rottweiler's life is when you first bring him home. For example, keeping your dog on a routine for eating (and therefore voiding) effectively makes your job easier. Because you will have a much better idea of when he needs to eliminate if you know the time of your Rottie's last meal, you can then take him to his appropriate elimination spot when he is most likely to relieve himself. By placing your dog on a feeding schedule, you thus save yourself time and frustration, and you also increase your dog's chance of success with housetraining.

Schedules can benefit both you and your dog in other ways, as well. Being part of a well-oiled routine can help make your dog feel more secure in his new environment and effectively prevent problems such as separation anxiety, which can manifest itself through annoying behaviors like excessive barking and chewing. Dogs can be incredibly patient animals, but they (like many of us) are also creatures of habit. If your Rottie knows that you will be home most days as soon as it gets dark, you will likely find him waiting to go for his walk and play with his favorite toy with you when you walk through the door at this time.

Another important activity to include in your Rottweiler's schedule is daily exercise. By taking just 15 to 20 minutes each day to take your dog for a walk, you provide him with an opportunity to spend valuable time with you, socialize with other people and dogs along the way, and stay fit in the process. Because unreleased energy can also lead to behavior issues, regular walks and play sessions can help you and your dog avoid these unpleasant problems.

Daily exercise is an important part of your Rottie's routine.

Crate

Even a well-behaved dog can get into trouble when left alone for too long with so many tempting items at his disposal. A friend of mine once told me that he sees the crate as a way of helping his dogs to behave properly when he isn't home. He said that if he didn't crate his dogs and then arrived home to find his couch in tattered pieces, he would consider it as much his own fault as theirs. At this point, I still wasn't sold on the practice of crating, though. To put it bluntly, I viewed the process as locking my dog in a jail cell, and I'm afraid to say I thought my friend (who for the sake of our friendship shall remain nameless) was just being lazy. I mean, if you just make the effort to train your dog, you won't have to deal with strewn garbage or chewed table legs—right? So I thought.

It wasn't until I realized that the crate (also called a kennel) can actually be an integral part of the training process did I learn how wrong I was. When my dog, Molly, began gnawing on the computer cords under my desk, I finally decided to give the crate a try—just while I was working and unable to properly supervise her. (Incidentally, it worked great, but that's a topic for another chapter.) Fortunately, I chose a model that worked perfectly for our particular needs, but this was largely a matter of luck, since I spent very little time researching and comparison shopping.

SENIOR DOG TIP

Making a New Home a Sweet Home

Perhaps you adopted your Rottweiler from your local humane society, or maybe you inherited a friend or relative's dog. Whatever your Rottie's history, if you have assumed the care of an older dog, he will go through a period of adjustment as he acclimates to his new home with you. Understandably, this transition may take several weeks or even months. Remain patient during the process, and be sure to spend extra time with him to help make the transition easier.

Types of Crates

Although many crates look alike, some major differences exist. Which crate is best for your dog depends on a few key issues.

Plastic Crates

Hard plastic crates are ideal for dogs who will be traveling by air with their owners. Airlines have a stringent policy of only allowing animals to fly in these rigid-style carriers. The plastic variety also offers a fair amount of privacy for a dog, which may be

*Stainless steel food and
water bowls are the safest
and most versatile.*

important if you want this item to serve as a quiet retreat for your pet. Plastic is more vulnerable to chewing, however, and usually takes up more space when being stored.

Wire Crates

Wire crates, although usually more expensive, offer dogs a 360-degree view of their surroundings. An owner can always toss a blanket across part of the enclosure for added privacy if desired. Wire crates typically break down even further than their plastic equivalents, making it possible to store the entire crate in a very narrow space. I personally find wire crates to be a bit complicated to assemble, but this could be due to my laughable shortcomings when it comes to that daunting phrase— "assembly required."

Crate Size

Once you decide which style is right for your dog, the next most important consideration is size. Don't be fooled into thinking that, because your Rottweiler puppy will grow to be such a large dog, he needs the biggest crate possible. Although he will need a crate designated large or extra-large (approximately 48 inches [121.9 cm] long), believe it or not, even bigger

models are available for such gargantuan breeds as the Saint Bernard and Great Dane. You may think that you are doing your dog a favor by affording him with a crate fit for one of these king-sized canines, but this isn't the case. Your Rottweiler should be able to stand comfortably and turn around in his crate, but having a superfluous amount of space will negate all the kennel's housetraining advantages. Too big is definitely better than too small, though, so don't hesitate to go with the larger version if your choices are either that or an intermediate model.

Food and Water Bowls

Feeding dishes may seem like one of the easiest items to check off your shopping list. After all, most dog dishes are the same, right? Wrong! The choices are surprisingly expansive, and not all bowls provide the same advantages. Some may even pose a health risk to your pet.

Plastic Bowls

Buy a plastic bowl for your Rottweiler puppy and you will likely be replacing it before your dog is even a year old. This is because plastic is the most vulnerable material when it comes to inappropriate chewing. Another unpleasant liability that arises from your dog's use of plastic bowls is the possibility of your dog suffering from plastic dish dermatitis, a condition that can cause your dog's nose and lips to lose their dark pigment—or worse, cause inflammation and soreness.

Ceramic Bowls

Ceramic bowls certainly aren't as susceptible to the whims of a teething puppy, but they will shatter into pieces if accidentally dropped or kicked around by a hungry Rottweiler. More important, though, many ceramic dishes pose the serious threat of lead poisoning. Because ceramic bowls made for animals are not yet held to the same standards as those constructed for human use, avoid ceramic pet dishes altogether. If you prefer to use ceramic dishes, purchase a set made for people instead. These should be labeled "high fire" or "table quality."

Stainless Steel Bowls

The most versatile dishes for nearly any breed are those made of stainless steel. Virtually indestructible, these metal bowls will withstand daily use and washing without subjecting your dog to any unnecessary ailments from the material's ingredients. For the sake of convenience, though, I do recommend purchasing two sets, so clean dishes are always waiting while the other two are being washed. Merely topping off your dog's dishes (even after emptying and rinsing) will expose him to the countless forms of bacteria that can accumulate on dishes left out all the time.

The Expert Knows

License and Registration, Please

In addition to providing your dog with a unique identification number in the event that he is ever lost, dog licenses are also required by law. Although fees are nominal, you will pay even less to register your dog if he has been neutered. (Remember to bring written proof from your veterinarian.) Check with your local municipality for individual prices and other necessary documents that you may need to provide during the licensing process.

FAMILY-FRIENDLY TIP

Keeping Involvement Age-Appropriate

Although a child can certainly play a large role in your Rottweiler's life, you must be careful not to let your Rottie's upbringing fall entirely on the shoulders of a young person. Two of a Rottweiler's most important needs are structure and discipline, concepts that most children are still in the process of learning themselves. For example, a well-intended child may simply get carried away with the fun of taking the family dog for a walk and forget the inherent purpose of teaching him how to walk properly—without pulling or biting at the leash. By accompanying your child while she literally takes the lead during this activity, though, you can instill the value of dog training in your child while making sure that all aspects of the task are being accomplished.

Gate

Whether you purchase a puppy or adopt an older Rottweiler, a pet gate (also called a baby gate) can be one of the most versatile items you will ever own. In the beginning, you will find that a gate can instantly create a safe environment for your new pet by keeping him out of reach of household dangers. Gates are also practical for feeding time if your household consists of multiple pets or for protecting your older dog from accidents such as falling down stairs.

Bear in mind that not just any gate will do for this larger breed. Shorter or flimsy models will do nothing to protect your dog; on the contrary, gates that may work fine for toy breeds can actually cause an injury to your dog if he scales it. You will probably pay a little more for your Rottweiler's gate, but rest assured that investing in this one pricier item will be less expensive than buying the smaller model first and then replacing it later.

The design you choose will depend on a variety of circumstances—including where you wish to use the gate and whether you want to install permanent hardware. Spring-mounted models can be used in virtually unlimited areas, provided that the gate is wide enough to span the distance between walls or doorways. Gates that swing open to allow you to walk through can be extremely convenient, but they require that you mount hinges to your woodwork to allow this recurring movement. Usually, though, these models are stronger than the moveable varieties.

Grooming Supplies

Most people assume that grooming a Rottweiler is a fairly simple task, and they'd be right. Although the Rottie is anything but a low-maintenance dog when it comes to nearly every other area, grooming is thankfully one aspect of this breed that requires only a moderate amount of time and effort. Still, a few important tools will be necessary. The worst grooming mistake you can make is to overlook the few simple tasks that must be done regularly to keep your friend in tip-top shape.

Because your dog's nails should be trimmed every week or two, one of the first things you'll need is a good pair of pliers-type toenail clippers. You will also need a slicker brush, a metal comb, and a shedding blade. (Although the Rottie's coat is relatively easy to maintain, daily brushing during seasonal shedding times is important if you don't want hair all over your home.)

Identification

We've all seen the homemade fliers tacked desperately to the bulletin boards of our local pet supply stores: Lost! Have you seen this dog? The details vary, but the plea is always sadly familiar. Like many of you, I usually spend a moment studying the photograph and then another thanking my lucky stars that

my own dogs are at home, safe and sound. But what if they weren't? What if your Rottweiler, like so many of these missing pets, managed to sneak out through the door? Or worse, what if he were stolen? Does your dog wear an identification tag with all the necessary information that would help a kind stranger return him to you?

Tags

Affixing your Rottweiler's collar with a tag bearing your name and contact information is a great start. Most pet supply stores now sell custom-engraved charms in cute designs and shapes, like bones and fire hydrants. The costs are reasonable, and in most cases, you can leave with the finished

A tattoo is a permanent form of identification for your pet.

product that same day. Some even offer self-serve machines.

Tattoos

If your pet is ever stolen, an ID tag will usually be the first thing the perpetrator tosses. In this kind of situation, you need a more permanent form of identification. At one time, tattoos were the best means of permanently identifying an animal, but as many owners have realized the hard way, even this seemingly indelible mark can be altered. A better option is to microchip your pet.

Microchips

Inserted under your Rottweiler's skin in a procedure as quick and painless as a vaccination, a microchip is literally the size of a grain of rice. This small safeguard can make a huge difference in the lives of you and your dog. When read by a handheld device (used by most veterinarians and shelters), the chip provides all the necessary information to bring your dog home to you. This indispensable technology has reunited countless pets with their beloved owners and thwarted a considerable number of animal thefts since its introduction to the pet community.

Leash

The most important thing that an owner needs to know about buying a leash for her Rottweiler is the importance of using it. More than any other accessory, this one item could literally save your dog's life, so always attach it whenever your dog is outdoors and beyond the safety of a fence. Leashes are also required in virtually every community for walking your dog in most public places.

Because Rottweilers are so strong, you must choose a leash that's sturdy

Choose a leash that's sturdy enough to hold your powerful Rottie.

enough to hold this powerful breed—even when your dog is faced with a temptation to pull away from you. In the beginning, though, your Rottie puppy will need a lightweight leash to help him acclimate to using one. Nylon usually works best for this. Once he is accustomed to walking on a leash (also commonly called a lead), you should then transition him to a leather variety. This offers an ideal combination of strength and comfort.

Another option that many owners find convenient is an extendable leash. This reel-style lead (usually housed in a plastic handle) offers the versatility of several leashes in one, as it can extend or retract to various lengths, depending on your needs. If you are taking a walk down a crowded city street, for example, you can keep the leash short (say 6 feet [1.8 m] or less), but when visiting the dog park, you might give your Rottweiler a little extra space (perhaps 16 feet [4.9 m] or longer). If for any reason you decide that a shorter length is more appropriate, simply call your dog and shorten his roaming radius. The one time you should not use an extendable lead is when you are training your dog to walk properly on a leash, because this extra flexibility will likely only distract him from the task at hand. If you are teaching him to come to you, though, this can be an invaluable tool, especially if you are tackling the command without a training partner.

Doggy Daycare

If you spend a large amount of time away from home, you may want to consider enlisting the help of a doggy daycare facility. Like daycare for human children, the best doggy daycare facilities strive to provide a safe and stimulating environment while exposing your dog to other dogs, as well as other human caregivers—both important components in proper socialization. When evaluating a daycare facility, request a tour, and ask as many questions as possible. Ensure that the business is adequately staffed (at least one caregiver for every ten dogs), and ask about protocol for issues such as discipline (this should never be physical) and emergencies. A responsible daycare business won't allow smaller dogs to play freely with larger ones, and some criteria should be in place for admission based on health and temperament. Don't worry about appearing demanding. You will be leaving your beloved dog with these people, so you should be comfortable with your choice.

Pens

From multi-panel x-pens (short for exercise pens) that collapse when not in use to heavier gauge enclosures with built-in doors, these are a great alternative to leaving your Rottweiler in his crate when you are nearby but cannot supervise him properly. While your Rottie is a puppy, a smaller x-pen may suffice, but he will quickly outgrow this small corral. If you plan to use the enclosure once your dog enters adulthood, a larger model is a wiser choice. Make sure that your puppy cannot squeeze through before leaving him unattended, but also look for a design that will be tall enough for your full-grown dog.

Toys

At first glance, most people assume that a Rottweiler's teeth will wreak havoc on most varieties of softer toys—and many are correct. With 320 pounds (145.1 kg) of bite pressure in their jaws (nearly three times that of human), Rotties can certainly destroy nearly anything in sight, a toy or otherwise. As one rescue worker explained to me, however, just because a dog can tear a toy to shreds doesn't mean he will. This worker makes a point of teaching her dogs to make the toy talk by using its squeaker, and she has found that Rotties, like so many other breeds, delight in this kind of play. So don't overlook the softer items when toy shopping for your Rottweiler! In addition to being fun, these items can help prevent your dog from developing a problematic chewing habit.

For those times when you cannot play with your dog, hard rubber toys that can be stuffed with an edible treat are a great way to entertain this intelligent breed. (Nearly empty plastic peanut butter jars can serve as an inexpensive substitute.) My dogs adore balls that dispense pieces of kibble when rolled a certain way.

So-called indestructible balls are also practical options for Rotties, as they may inadvertently destroy softer versions when in the midst of a passionate game of fetch. Try to avoid tennis balls, however, as these can accidentally pose a choking hazard for this larger breed. Some Rottweilers have actually been known to swallow tennis balls, causing serious obstructions. This warning may be applied to other smaller toys as well, so always make sure the size is right. Rottweilers bore very easily, so providing them with stimulating activities as opposed to idle playthings is essential in keeping them from developing destructive behaviors. Even if you crate your Rottie when you are away from home or cannot fully supervise him, there is undeniable value in averting him from constant chewing. No dog should be crated for more than a few hours at a time, and you will be amazed by how quickly a Rottweiler can reduce your coffee table to toothpicks—sometimes in as little time as it takes for you to start preparing dinner. So avoid this kind of habit before it starts!

Your Rottweiler's initial shopping list may seem extensive, but most of these items will only need to be purchased once. Selecting quality items will help ensure that you won't need to replace anything. Once your dog has everything he needs, you will likely find that shopping for more superfluous items occasionally can be fun. You can make it even more enjoyable by taking your dog along with you to pick out any new belongings. Safety must always be your first priority, but to your dog, there's nothing like the smell of a brand-new chew toy—or the time spent with you to go get it.

Chapter 3

Good Eating

Our dogs benefit from eating right just as much as we do, yet many owners overlook the importance of good canine nutrition, just as they often allow their own nutritional priorities to slip. In this often frantically busy world, it is much easier to buzz through a drive-thru than prepare a simple, healthy meal. Likewise, picking up a bag of supermarket dog food is more convenient than making a special trip to the pet supply store for a healthier alternative. Unfortunately, in both cases, prices may be paid for this time saved, including health problems like obesity, diabetes, and cancer that may be linked to inferior diets.

The feeding regimens we choose for our pets can have a profound effect on whether our faithful companions live long, healthy lives. This chapter gives you the tools to make an informed decision about the best diet for your Rottweiler.

Nutrients

Selecting the best diet for your dog can be an almost overwhelming task. With what appears to be countless choices, how can you decide which plan is the right one for your dog? A basic understanding of what every dog needs is a great place to begin when faced with this dilemma. The following is a list of nutrients that your dog needs or will encounter in his diet:

- carbohydrates
- fats
- minerals
- proteins
- vitamins
- water

Commercial Foods

Now that you know everything that your Rottweiler needs in his diet, finding the right food should be easy, right? Although it would be nice if finding the best food were indeed that simple, you still need to make a few additional decisions. Of the many different canine feeding regimens, one isn't necessarily better than any other, but one may indeed be better for your Rottweiler and your lifestyle.

Your Rottweiler needs a balanced diet to thrive.

Dry

Dry dog food is the most popular choice among owners, and it is easy to see why. With the many premium brands on the market today, you can provide your precious pet with a bowl full of high-quality nutrients without even getting your hands dirty. Dry kibble can be purchased in bulk, saving you both time and money, and it works for either a scheduled or free-feeding plan.

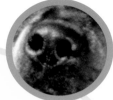

The Confusing World of Dog Food Labels

Before 1994, 40 percent of food in the United States was packaged without any nutritional labeling whatsoever. Fortunately, we have come a long way in recent years in changing this situation. The Food and Drug Administration (FDA) now requires that all manufacturers of human-grade products list the contents of every package, including a precise breakdown of the amounts of calories, fat, cholesterol, and sodium. Laws even exist pertaining to the use of nutritional claims. Canine food labeling has also undergone some recent changes, making it necessary for dog food manufacturers to list ingredients in descending order by weight. Unfortunately, much work is still to be done in making this new system an ideal one. The technical weight of any item includes the moisture within it, making it possible for an ingredient that is approximately 70 percent water (like chicken) to be listed first on the list. By learning to decipher your Rottweiler's dog food label, you can help him avoid malnutrition and live a longer, happier life.

Canned

Although canned versions of most dry foods are available, they offer both benefits and liabilities. Overwhelmingly, the biggest advantage of wet food is its appeal to dogs. Many wet foods have extremely pleasing aromas and simply must taste good—as evidenced by the number of dogs I know who come running at the mere sound of a can opener. Canned foods may be stored even longer than bags of kibble, but once opened, they must be consumed right away. Leftovers may be refrigerated to prevent spoilage, but even then they only last a day or two. (Always allow food to return to room temperature before serving the second time.) The biggest problem with wet food, though, is the havoc it can wreak with your Rottweiler's dental health if an effort is not made to brush his teeth frequently enough. Dogs eating canned foods are substantially more prone to plaque and tartar than their kibble-munching friends.

Semi-Moist

Semi-moist foods may at first seem like a reasonable middle ground for the owners who want to provide their dogs with good taste and sound nutrition, but most of these foods are so high in sugar that they are actually more problematic than wetter varieties. If you find the burger-like shapes of these preservative-rich foods appealing, consider giving your dog real, lean hamburger or ground turkey instead. It would be a lot healthier and probably tastier, too.

Dry food is the most popular choice among dog owners.

Noncommercial Foods

One of the best ways for you to ensure that your Rottweiler is getting the right balance of nutrients is to make his meals yourself. Prepared foods, by definition, must contain a certain amount of preservatives and other ingredients that you may find less desirable as you learn more about canine nutrition. The key here is to educate yourself thoroughly before starting a noncommercial diet regimen, especially if your dog will be eating this kind of food exclusively.

Home-Cooked Diet

Home-cooked canine diets have been around for centuries, but in recent years, they have evolved from tossing the family's leftovers to the dog to preparing an individual portion just for

him. Although preparing a home-cooked diet may initially seem expensive, cooking for your pet can actually be even more economical than buying a quality pre-packaged food. If you shop the sales or visit a butcher, you might hardly notice a difference in your overall expenditure. By planning ahead and cooking some entrees at the beginning of each week, you can even save time as well as cash.

The biggest downfall to home cooking is the effort you must make in doing your homework. Because your dog will be deriving all his nutrients from the meals you select for the menu, you must consistently meet all his needs. You must also be careful not to provide too much of any nutrient that in excess could be harmful to his health. The best way to make sure that you haven't overlooked anything is to speak with your veterinarian before beginning such a regimen. She may also be able to point you toward other useful resources for this endeavor.

One of the easiest ways to ensure that your dog's diet isn't lacking in a particular nutrient is by supplementing his home-cooked meals with a small amount of prepackaged food. This is also an excellent way to transition him to a home-cooked plan. I personally do just the opposite—that is, I feed my own dogs primarily kibble, but I supplement the dry food with an occasional home-cooked treat. The beauty of this kind of regimen is that it can be altered to suit virtually any dog or owner's lifestyle.

Raw Diet

Considerable debate continues among dog owners about whether feeding raw foods is a good idea. Many Rottweiler breeders and owners—and even a fair number of veterinarians—feel strongly that feeding a raw diet (commonly called the BARF diet, an acronym for Bones and Raw Foods) is the best way to provide a dog with the nutrition that his canine body needs. Inarguably, raw foods retain certain nutritional properties that cooking destroys. It is also a well-known fact that wild dogs have eaten raw meat for centuries with few resulting problems.

Like home cooking, feeding raw foods doesn't have to stress your budget. In addition to basing your shopping lists on the weekly sales flyers, you can also save a great deal of money by freezing raw foods or purchasing prepackaged raw canine meals that are already frozen. With this latter option, you get the proverbial best of both worlds—the benefits of a raw diet but without any of the hassle. Because these packages can be large and cumbersome, however, having an extra freezer in your home is definitely a plus.

It is important to note that raw food is certainly not limited to meat. Other raw foods included in this plan are eggs, fish, fruit, and vegetables. All these offer unique health-enhancing benefits when served uncooked. Like home cooking, a successful raw diet must be properly balanced to offer its undeniable advantages.

FAMILY-FRIENDLY TIP

Little Helpers

Small children are simply too unpredictable to involve them directly in the feeding process, but they can be included in other ways. Perhaps yours can help by carrying a can from the cupboard to the counter or by calling the animal to dinner. As your child gets a bit older, allow her to offer treats to the dog as a way of introducing her to a more involved role in the feeding process.

To receive the benefits of certain foods, it may also be necessary to grind or blend them before serving.

So why all the controversy? One of the most common concerns among naysayers of the BARF diet is the list of threats posed by bones. Chicken bones, in particular, which have a tendency to splinter, put a dog at increased risk for choking or suffering intestinal ruptures or blockages. Although smaller breeds are certainly more prone to this kind of accident, any dog can experience one or more of these problems. Additionally, eating raw meat means an elevated risk of coming into contact with dangerous bacteria, such as *Salmonella* and *Escherichia coli*.

If, after weighing the risks, you decide to try a raw diet, again, discuss your choice with your veterinarian, who can help address any issues you may have overlooked. Also, be sure to use the same precautions when feeding your Rottie as you do when cooking meat for your family: Wash hands and surfaces thoroughly after coming into contact with any raw meat to avoid cross-contamination.

Free Feeding Versus Scheduled Feeding

To some dog owners, the choice between free feeding and schedule feeding is a no-brainer. To others, though, the decision isn't as obvious. If you are fortunate enough to have a healthy dog who knows when to say when, free feeding (leaving food available to your dog at all times) may not pose any problems whatsoever. If, on the other hand, your dog (like mine) would eat his way clear to the other side of the dog food bag if given half the chance, scheduling his meals may be a much more prudent option.

Feeding home-cooked or raw foods requires research to ensure that your dog is getting a balanced diet.

SENIOR DOG TIP

Like Fine Kibble

As your Rottweiler gets older, you will need to tailor his diet to his changing needs. This should include transitioning to a food rich in protein—20 to 30 percent is usually ideal, because older dogs require more of this vital nutrient. Always check with your veterinarian before making any big dietary change, though, because dogs afflicted with heart or kidney problems typically need less protein, as well as less phosphorus and sodium. If your aging companion is in good overall health, a high-quality senior diet may match his needs perfectly, but this doesn't mean that he will necessarily find it appetizing. In fact, boredom with food is a common problem among older dogs.

One way to combat the monotony is to opt for a wet or canned food, which usually affords a more enticing aroma and provides the added advantage of being gentler on your dog's teeth and gums. Because wet food leaves your pet more susceptible to plaque and tartar, be sure to keep his toothbrush around and stock up on the canine toothpaste.

Like people, dogs can also suffer from constipation more frequently as they get older. To help avoid this problem, select a food high in fiber (approximately 3 to 5 percent), or add wheat bran to your dog's daily meals. Or you may also offer soluble fiber in the form of such healthy snacks as oatmeal, oranges, or brussels sprouts.

If your Rottweiler is ever sick, you have certain advantages to knowing how much he has eaten and when. Especially if other dogs live in your home, it may even take you longer to realize that your Rottie is ill if he is on a free-feeding regimen because a change in appetite is one of the first symptoms of many health problems. Weight is also more easily managed through scheduled feedings.

Of course, some dogs thrive on a free-feeding plan. If this is the case for your Rottweiler, there is really no reason to change to a schedule. Perhaps you want to make sure that your dog has food available if you have to work late, or maybe you simply prefer being able to pour the kibble once a day. Just be sure to wash your dog's dishes daily, and always toss the food left over from the day before. Even dry food can spoil if left exposed to the air too long, and bacteria from the food and your dog's saliva can make your dog sick if left to accumulate.

It is considerably more difficult to transition a dog from free feeding to a schedule than the reverse, so take some time before ruling out the latter option. If you are in the midst of this challenging move, begin by dividing your dog's total food into several meals given throughout the day, and gradually lessen the number of feeding times until you have him on the schedule of your choice. Avoiding snacks during this period can also be helpful.

Obesity

When fed too liberally, Rottweilers are extremely susceptible to not only obesity but all the health problems that accompany it. And as anyone who has ever tried to take extra pounds (kg) off a Rottweiler can tell you, reducing a dog's weight is no easy

task. It involves a careful combination of reducing calories and increasing exercise, all based specifically on the individual animal's current health state.

Overweight Rottweilers are especially prone to a number of health problems and injuries, including high cholesterol, heart and lung issues, and hip and knee problems. Obesity can even affect temperament. The double edge of this sword is that the dog desperately needs to lose his extra weight, but the new owner must be careful to pace his exercise routine appropriately. Pushing an already overweight animal to exercise too intensely or for too long can be downright dangerous. If you are ready to help your Rottweiler get back into shape, ask your vet to help you create the best strategy for your dog.

Few things affect a dog's health more than a nutritionally sound diet. Fortunately, you have many ways to accomplish this important goal. Whether you choose to feed your dog a high-quality commercial diet or prepare him a variety of fresh foods daily, you can help your Rottweiler remain fit and healthy by making his diet a top priority.

Your Rottie should have access to cool, fresh water at all times.

Treating Your Rottweiler Right

Pet owners have always liked to show their animal family a little extra love with the occasional treat, but modern treats have gone way beyond slipping Rover a little turkey under the kitchen table. These days, pet owners can visit pet bakeries, buy frozen dog desserts at the grocery store, or make homemade treats from a pet-treat cookbook. With all these options, how do you know the right thing to feed your pet? Here are some tips:

- Buy treats made specifically for your kind of pet. Most pet stores now offer treats formulated for all kinds of animals. These treats are designed to taste good to your pet without upsetting his stomach or throwing his diet out of whack.
- If your Rottweiler eats at scheduled mealtimes, don't let him fill up on treats before meals.
- Try giving your Rottweiler treats that benefit his health. Pet stores now offer dental treats that clean teeth; treats with added vitamins, minerals, and antioxidants; and more.
- If you're longing to let your dog sample a little human food but don't want to expand her waistline, you can try giving her a few fresh vegetables. Dogs often love veggies like carrots, broccoli, and green beans, which are low in calories and high in vitamins and healthy fiber. You'll have to use some care, however. Some produce that people love can be harmful to dogs. Onions cause anemia, for example, and grapes and raisins can be toxic. Don't feed your dog any new or unusual veggies without consulting your veterinarian.
- When you give your Rottweiler treats, add up the number of calories in the treats, then subtract that from the number of calories he gets from his regular food that day.
- In general, don't let treats make up more than 10 percent of your Rottweiler's diet.

As for the gourmet yummies available, use your best judgment when deciding what to give your pet. Check what ingredients they're made from and how much fat they contain. If your dog is healthy, and his overall diet is balanced, the occasional extravagant snack won't do him any harm.

(Courtesy of AAHA and Healthypet.com)

Looking Good

Grooming a Rottweiler may seem like a rather straightforward task. While this assumption is mostly accurate, owners must be careful not to mistake ease of grooming for no need for grooming at all. Having a short-haired dog means carrying out virtually all the same tasks as you would with a fluffier canine—just with less time focused on his fur.

Because few people want to wrestle with a 100-pound (45.4 kg) dog to clip a single toenail, it is a good idea to introduce your Rottie to the grooming process as early as possible. Also, by staying on top of all grooming tasks, you will help your dog look and feel great. He may even grow to enjoy it!

Being clean and properly groomed is also a huge factor in canine health. As those who have skipped grooming altogether have learned the hard way, a regrettable chain of events follow putting off these important steps. Dogs with fleas, for example, itch. Dogs who itch frequently develop hot spots, sore patches of red skin that the dog simply cannot resist scratching. Once this happens, an infection can soon follow. The story remains essentially the same for any important task an owner ignores.

That Coat Runs Skin Deep

The simple truth is that a dog cannot do some things for himself. Sure, your Rottweiler may self-groom several times a day, but he cannot brush his own coat or bathe himself. This section will teach you how to do just that.

Brushing

The best part of brushing a Rottweiler is that it requires very little instruction. Unlike a Poodle or a Cocker Spaniel, there is nothing daunting about brushing out a Rottie—no sectioning of

Grooming contributes to your Rottweiler's overall health.

hair before you begin, no knots or tangles to remove, and no complicated hairstyle to maintain. In fact, your dog won't look much different when you finish—but don't let this fool you. He will be better for it each and every time.

As most of us know, dogs are very adept self groomers. My dog Molly is especially meticulous about cleaning her feet. No matter how many times she goes outside during a given day, she invariably cleans her paws after every trip. Perhaps you think this is evidence that she does not really need my help. After all, even when I give her a bath, she follows up and cleans herself anyway. While I joke about this regularly, it is vital that I remember how the fact that Molly is so particular about her hygiene makes it even more important that I brush her regularly. By brushing away the dead skin, hair, and other debris she picks up from the ground and floor, I am reducing her risk of ingesting these questionable substances.

Perhaps less important, but still a challenge for many owners, shedding also becomes much less of a problem when you brush your Rottie regularly. (Once a week is ideal.) Rottweilers are surprisingly prolific shedders. Technically, the breed is supposed to shed twice a year (in the spring and fall), but because of most dogs' exposure to artificial light, they can actually shed year-round, with only slight differences seasonally. When you brush the dead hair away during grooming, you lessen the amount you need to sweep and vacuum from your floors and carpeting or brush off your furniture and clothing. A shedding blade may also come in handy for this purpose.

How to Brush Your Rottie
Begin by brushing your Rottweiler's coat gently with a soft-bristled brush.

Although his hair won't tangle like a longer-haired breed, it is still essential that you reach your Rottie's skin, because dead hair and other debris must be removed. Always brush in the direction of hair growth, and be careful not to bear down too hard. Remember, you want to reach the skin, not scratch it.

Remember to always brush your dog before bathing. With longer-haired breeds, the primary reason for this is to avoid making any tangles worse. Obviously, this is not an issue for the Rottweiler, but the dead skin and hair (and the debris surrounding it) should also be removed before you wash your pet. This will help you get him truly clean.

Bathing
Even if your Rottie is the outdoorsy type, he shouldn't need a bath as often as his longer-haired friends. Unless your dog has decided to bask in a mud bath

Grooming Supplies

Your Rottie's grooming bag needn't be big, but every properly groomed Rottweiler needs a few particular items:
- canine toothpaste and toothbrush (or gauze)
- ear cleaning solution
- moisturizing shampoo
- nail clippers
- soft-bristled brush and metal comb

of his own, bathing with shampoo should only be necessary about every other month. Some owners even prefer stretching baths out to every six months—with only a simple sponge bath or two given sporadically between these times. This is a personal choice. As long as your dog is clean and healthy, how often you bathe him is up to you. One thing you may have heard that is untrue is that you shouldn't bathe your dog too often. Within reason, you can give your Rottie a bath as often as once or twice a month, provided that you are using a quality shampoo appropriate for his coat and skin type and rinsing thoroughly after each shampoo. If you show your dog in conformation, for example, you will want him looking and smelling his best for each event that he attends.

When choosing a shampoo, look for a moisturizing variety. This will help replace any natural oils stripped away during the bathing process. Most important, never use your own shampoo on your dog.

Because the pH of a dog's skin differs so dramatically from that of a human's skin (ours is considerably more acidic), treating your dog to your salon-brand shampoo will only dry out his skin. If you wish to indulge your pet with special pampering products, you can find these items at your local pet supply store.

In addition to the moisturizing varieties, a number of other specialized shampoos are on the market. From color-enhancing formulas to sweet-smelling botanical varieties, there is

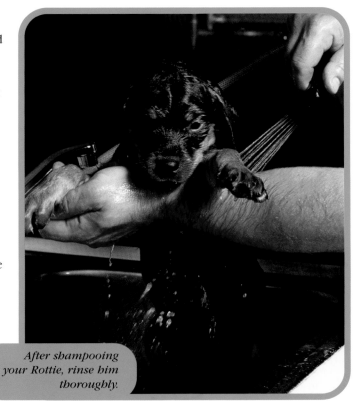

After shampooing your Rottie, rinse him thoroughly.

hardly a kind of shampoo a dog owner cannot find. (One very famous human hair care guru has even launched a line of pet-care products.)

If your Rottweiler suffers from dry skin or dandruff, follow up shampooing with a quality conditioner. These, too, are available in a full array of specialized varieties.

If your dog is fearful of water, or if you have a hard time managing your dog in the bathtub, waterless shampoos provide a convenient alternative to conventional washing. These powder-like shampoos do require extensive brushing, but they can come in quite handy during colder months or following a surgical procedure.

How to Bathe Your Rottie

Once you have retrieved everything you will need for your Rottweiler's bath, you should then draw the tub. Tepid water is best; if you are unsure whether the temperature is too hot or cold, that old trick of dipping an elbow into the water works just as well now as it did when we were all babies. Apply the shampoo to your hands first, rubbing them together to create a fine lather before soaping your dog's back. From his back, you should then move to his legs, chest, belly, and bottom—and don't forget his feet. As important as washing your dog is, the most essential step comes next: rinsing. After rinsing your dog's coat thoroughly, go back and rinse him one more time. This simple

FAMILY-FRIENDLY TIP

Should Grooming Be a Family Affair?

The best way to include children in the dog grooming process is to start while the dog is young. Because your Rottweiler puppy won't require as much coifing as many other breeds, it is even more vital that you let your child play a part each time you perform a specific task. If the child is young, you may want to limit her job to dispensing the shampoo during a bath or passing you the cotton balls when you are cleaning your Rottie's ears. Older kids can be instructed to handle more complicated tasks.

If your Rottweiler is older and has an aversion to grooming, however, you should wait to involve your children in the process until you have helped your dog over this hurdle. In some cases, a dog will still ultimately prefer to leave the grooming responsibilities to you alone, his trusted owner. If your Rottie is on the shy side, respect his preference to not have an audience.

step will help prevent unnecessary itching and drying of your dog's skin once the bath is done.

Nail Care

If you can hear your dog's toenails when he walks across the floor, they are already too long. Overgrown nails can break or tear, which can expose the nail bed, that sensitive area within the nail. Even more painful is having a nail pulled completely out if it gets caught on something such as clothing or carpeting—an accident that can also leave your Rottie extremely susceptible to infection. Nails left to grow too long can also scratch; your dog can hurt both himself and other household members with these talon-like claws.

The best way to help your dog tolerate nail trimming as an adult is to start early and remain consistent, trimming nails weekly as soon as you bring your puppy home. Some owners find that nails on the front feet grow faster than those on the back; if this is the case for your dog, you may find it adequate to only trim the nails on his hind feet every other week. Handle your Rottie's feet as often as

possible, whether it's time for nail trimming or not. This will help him become more comfortable when it's time for his trim.

One important factor to consider before trimming the nails is what kind of nail clippers to use. Many owners of large dogs find guillotine-style clippers difficult to maneuver because the nail itself must be placed inside the guide hole before snipping it. Even with larger clippers, this can be challenging. Scissors-style clippers can also be problematic.

The Expert Knows

A Healthy Dose of Grooming

Just as our doctors encourage us to examine our own bodies for any suspicious changes, we should also check our pets regularly for any abnormalities, and grooming time is one of the best opportunities for this. When most of us think of performing a health check, our minds go straight to what we fear most—a cancerous lump. While finding a tumor before it grows into a bigger threat is certainly important, it is only one part of this potentially life-saving process. When examining your Rottweiler, look for anything that is out of the ordinary, like skin rashes, cuts or scrapes (commonly found on a dog's paw pads), or any foreign bodies such as fleas or ticks. If you find anything unusual, talk to your vet to see if this change could signal a health problem. Remember, you know your dog best, so you will likely pick up on the first signs of illness before anyone else.

Although this design can sometimes be used on dogs, scissors typically work best on smaller breeds. The best option for a larger dog like the Rottie is usually a pliers-style clipper. Resembling a small pair of pruning shears, these clippers allow maximum visibility of the area you are cutting and generally work very effectively even on thicker nails. Whatever style you choose, select a heavy-duty trimmer, and keep it sharp. For guillotine-style clippers, this means replacing the blade regularly. For scissors or pliers-style trimmers, routine sharpening will be necessary. And don't forget to pick up a container of styptic powder to stash in your medicine cabinet, just in case you accidentally cut the nail bed (also called the quick).

Begin nail trimming when your Rottie is a puppy, because this will make it easier to trim his nails as an adult.

How to Trim Your Rottie's Nails

To avoid the quick, trim just a small portion of the nail more often, as opposed to clipping longer lengths less frequently. This gradual method has been shown to actually cause the quick to recede, making your dog less vulnerable to accidental cuts during the nail-trimming process. In dogs with dark-colored nails, the pinkish-looking nail bed can be difficult to distinguish. If you do nip the quick, don't panic. Apply pressure to the wound with a sterile towel soaked in cold water. If the bleeding persists, you may use a styptic pencil, pad, or powder to speed clotting. Other items that may be substituted include a soft bar of soap, cornstarch, or a wet tea bag.

If you find yourself repeatedly skimming the quick, you may want to leave nail trimming to a professional. Professional dog groomers or veterinarians will usually trim a dog's nails for a nominal fee, and your Rottie will be spared the pain of unnecessary accidents. Recurring accidents may traumatize your dog and make the process even more difficult for both of you.

Ear Care

Ear cleaning isn't difficult, but fighting an ear infection that results from inattention to this important task can be arduous, requiring weeks or even months of treatment with antibiotics in the most severe cases. The best way to avoid this problem is to simply keep your dog's ears clean and free of debris. Although the Rottweiler's ears are certainly not long, they do hang over the opening to the ear canal, leaving him moderately susceptible to the kind of moist environment that breeds bacteria. For this reason, your dog's ears should be cleaned at least once weekly.

How To Care for Your Rottie's Ears

Many dogs do not like having their ears cleaned, but with a little preparation, you can make the process a relatively quick and certainly painless one. Before you begin cleaning your dog's ear, give it a quick sniff. A healthy ear shouldn't smell offensive. If either ear smells especially bad, skip the cleaning process altogether and schedule an appointment with your veterinarian to rule out an infection. Although you may be tempted to clean the ear before heading to your appointment, bear in mind that doing so may aggravate an area that is already irritated and sore. It can also impede your vet's ability to properly swab the area, an important step in diagnosing a problem. Other signs of a problem include redness, discharge, or pawing or scratching at the ear.

Bond, Grooming Bond

Most grooming tasks are considerably easier to accomplish once you have established your Rottweiler's trust. Just like a young child, your dog may at first be fearful of having his ears cleaned or his toenails trimmed. This pivotal introduction period can determine whether your dog remains hesitant of grooming or begins to see it as an experience with pampering potential. By taking the time to slowly but consistently acquaint your Rottie with the various aspects of grooming, you lessen his fears. Your dog isn't the only one benefiting from this special time, though. Beginning or ending each grooming session with a special treat will blur the lines between a monotonous responsibility and a fun one for both of you. No rule says that grooming has to be a one-dimensional job, so massage your pet before his bath, offer him a kiss or a cookie after cleaning his eyes, or sing to him as you brush his teeth. And never forget to tell your dog how beautiful he is. The best way to establish that all-important trust is by approaching every activity as a bonding opportunity.

If the ear appears healthy, next use a cleaner that is alcohol free. This will help avoid any burning within the ear. Squirt a small amount of the solution into your dog's ear and then simply rub the ear from the outside to loosen any matter within it. Although many dogs hate the squirting process, most delight in the ear rub that follows. Once you have moved the cleaner all around, use cotton balls (never swabs, as they can damage the inner ear) to wipe the ear clean. Because a dog's ear canal is L-shaped, you will not likely puncture the ear drum during this process, but

When cleaning your dog's ears, take care never to push anything into his ear canal.

do be gentle, and don't reach too far inside the ear. Keep wiping the area until the cotton comes out mostly clean. Bear in mind that a small amount of wax is good for the ear, so don't expect the cotton to remain pristinely white. Too much rubbing can also irritate an ear.

Finally, never pull hair from your dog's ears. Although hair can impede air flow into your dog's ears, ripping it out can be painful. It can also expose your dog to a nasty infection.

Eye Care

Caring for your Rottweiler's eyes is probably one of the easiest of all grooming tasks. Just like the others, though, it should never be ignored.

How often your Rottie's eyes need cleaning depends somewhat on the individual animal. Some dogs produce significantly more eye debris than others, but most only need cleaning about once a week.

How to Care for Your Rottie's Eyes

Simply wiping the area around the eye with a wet cloth is all that needs to be done. This helps to remove any debris that has collected in this area. Allowing

this matter to accumulate leaves your dog more prone to infections such as conjunctivitis (pink eye).

While wiping your dog's eyes, make a point of inspecting the area for anything out of the ordinary. Scratches, cloudiness, extreme redness, or excessive discharge are all causes for concern and should be addressed with your dog's veterinarian. While Rotties are not especially prone to eye problems, any problem that is found early has a better chance of not becoming a more serious issue. For this reason, it is a good preventive measure to have your dog examined by a veterinary ophthalmologist at least once every few years. To locate a canine ophthalmologist in your area, visit the American College of Veterinary Ophthalmologists (ACVO) at www.acvo.com.

Dental Care

Good dental care is easily overlooked, but a dog with atrocious breath and teeth caked with tartar is impossible to ignore. Unfortunately, poor dental care is more than offensive—it's downright dangerous to your pet's health. The bacteria that accumulate in your dog's mouth are transported to all other areas of his body. Dogs suffering from tooth decay and gingivitis are at an increased risk of suffering from countless other afflictions, including coronary heart disease and general mortality.

How often should you brush? Ideally, you should try to brush your Rottie's teeth every day. If this isn't possible, don't simply give up on the task because you can't adhere to such a stringent schedule. Brush as often as you can. If you can't brush as often as you'd like, though, try to avoid soft foods that cause plaque and tartar to accumulate more quickly.

How to Care for Your Rottie's Teeth

We've all seen the conventional canine toothbrush kit sold in most pet supply stores. Although this is certainly a great all-in-one way to get everything you need to maintain your Rottweiler's dental health, believe it or not, even the toothbrush is not necessary. If your Rottie balks at the idea of inserting a brush into his mouth, simply take a piece of white gauze soaked in tepid water and brush your dog's teeth with your gauze-covered finger. As he warms to the idea of having a foreign object in his mouth, you may add the brush at a

SENIOR DOG TIP

Keep That Grooming Appointment!

Even the simplest grooming tasks require a little extra time and patience as your Rottweiler moves into his senior years. If your dog suffers from arthritis, for example, you may need to be a little gentler when handling his feet for nail trims. Likewise, he may develop some harmless albeit inconvenient lumps and bumps that make brushing a bit trickier. (Always have any new growth checked by your veterinarian to make sure that it is indeed benign.) You may also find that your Rottie's dental care may require a more delicate approach if any of his teeth have broken, loosened, or decayed in recent years. The biggest grooming mistake the owner of an older dog can make is to skip these tasks altogether simply because they have become a greater challenge.

As your dog ages, continue with his complete grooming routine. Use this time to evaluate his growing needs, and pinpoint any issues that could affect his health. Perhaps it is time to ask your vet to remove any built-up tartar on your Rottie's teeth or to schedule a veterinary ophthalmologic exam to diagnose and treat any vision problems. By keeping on top of these tasks, you will help ensure that your Rottweiler remains as healthy as possible as he faces the trials of aging.

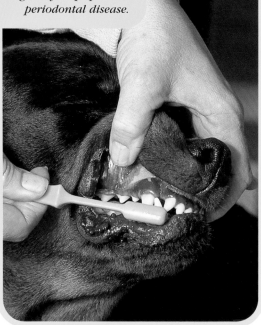

Brushing your dog's teeth regularly helps prevent periodontal disease.

Once you have applied some toothpaste to the gauze (or between the bristles of your brush, as opposed to just on top of them), brush your dog's teeth in an oval motion at a 45-degree angle, concentrating on the area where the teeth meet the gums. The area in need of the most attention is usually the outside of the upper teeth, but be sure to reach all your dog's teeth, both front and back. Because canine toothpaste doesn't need to be rinsed from your dog's mouth, you needn't worry about this step, although a refreshing drink of water is always a nice way to end the task. Above all else, be gentle in your approach and you will find that, in a short time, even a dog who hasn't been acclimated to this process will tolerate it surprisingly well.

The Adored—I Mean, Adorned—Rottweiler

I once knew a Rottweiler owner who painted her dog's toenails. The dog, named Brandi, would sit long enough for a complete pedicure and for the polish to dry afterward. Another Rottie I knew, this one named Abby, was less of a girly girl. She even relaxed in a doghouse when her owner was at work all day—a doghouse he had built especially for her that was wired with electricity so that she would have light and television while he was gone. All true.

later time, but this won't be a necessity. If you are getting the teeth clean, that's all that matters.

A good way to introduce your dog to tooth brushing is by offering him a taste of canine toothpaste. Because dogs cannot spit when brushing is finished, their toothpaste must be completely safe to swallow. (Human toothpaste, which contains ingredients that can upset your dog's stomach, shouldn't be swallowed, so never use it on your dog.) If your dog is anything like my own, you will win him over as soon as his nose gets a whiff of the tantalizing flavors available, such as chicken, beef, and liver.

The lengths we sometimes go to spoil our dogs can seem indulgent (or downright absurd) to those who don't understand our fierce love for these animals. One thing is certain, though. The pet supply industry has definitely caught on to our overwhelming urge to pamper our pooches, and the pet pampering business is a big one. But what items does your Rottweiler truly need?

Admittedly, many of the products available today are aimed more at the consumer than the dog himself. Cologne, for example, is in my opinion too hard on a canine nose. As someone with a sensitive nose myself, I can only imagine how torturous it must be for a dog to be spritzed with a fragrance that someone else selects and be forced to endure it all day. The best question to ask when selecting a product for your dog is this: How will this help my dog?

And perhaps even more important: Can it hurt him? If you can't answer the first question, or if you answer yes to the second, you should pass on the item no matter how cute it is.

One great product that I think is a must-have if your Rottweiler spends time outdoors is paw wax. Providing a thin layer of protection to your dog's feet, paw wax should be applied whenever your dog will be walking on any surface that can hurt his feet. This includes hot asphalt and gravel, as well as slippery surfaces such as ice and snow, for which paw wax also provides extra traction.

Whether your Rottie needs a coat really depends on the climate in which you live. To many Rottweiler owners, the idea of dressing a dog in a coat or sweater seems emasculating, but if your dog enjoys being outdoors in temperatures of lower than 32°F (0°C), he may appreciate the garment. Not all canine clothing is feminine in its appearance. A fleece or denim coat will keep your dog warm and allow him to maintain the rugged look that attracted you to him in the first place.

Whether your dog enjoys being pampered or simply accepts grooming as a part of his daily routine, you show him how much you love him each time you attend to his grooming needs. A clean Rottweiler not only looks better—he feels better. And nothing looks better than a happy dog.

49

Feeling Good

A healthy Rottweiler inspires the same kind of awe as a brawny human athlete. We see him, and we are instantly impressed. To maintain this striking exterior, owners must focus on keeping their dogs healthy both inside and out. Regular veterinary care, a smart diet, and regular exercise all play important roles in preserving this outwardly healthy appearance.

G ood health also helps keep your Rottie happy. A dog in pain or discomfort is more likely to shy away from such habits as exercising and eating, activities necessary to help him through periods of ailing health. A sick dog is even more likely to suffer from emotional problems, such as depression. Essentially, a physically fit animal looks good in large part because he feels good.

Finding a Vet

Next to you, your veterinarian will have a more significant effect on your dog's health than anyone else. If your dog is sick or injured, you want to know that he is in capable hands—especially when his needs surpass your own knowledge and abilities. For this reason, you must find the best possible person for the job.

Ask Questions

Although the world of veterinary medicine has changed significantly over the last few decades, one thing remains the same: Old-fashioned word of mouth is still usually the best way to find a good veterinarian. Unlike flashy telephone book ads, talking with your friends and neighbors can yield the kind of information that simply can't be summarized in an advertisement.

One of the first things you'll want to know is whether a potential vet is familiar with large breeds in particular. Some of my best friends are so-called cat people, but when selecting a person to oversee my dog's medical care, I would rather choose someone who has an affinity for the canine population. My own dogs seem to know when someone truly likes them, and I think this has a

Choose a vet who is knowledgeable about large-breed dogs and Rottweilers in particular.

genuine effect on their comfort level with an individual.

Stop in for a Visit

Once you have someone specific in mind, stop by (with or without your dog) to set up an appointment to meet the vet and her staff. This quick preliminary visit can give you an idea of what a typical day is like at this vet's office. Be patient while the staff assists the clients who arrive for their appointments, and use this time to take in all the outward details of their experiences. Is the staff friendly? Do they seem familiar with and knowledgeable about each animal's situation? You may even strike up a conversation with one of the clients while in the waiting room. Keep it casual, but remember to read between the lines. Those who are less than satisfied with their pets' level of care probably won't be very forthcoming in this setting, but those who have been particularly pleased will often bubble over with just the kind of information you need.

Also, look around for signs that the hospital is a caring and professional environment. Do the doctors and support staff interact in a positive manner? Are enough people available to properly handle the workload? Are the pets welcomed with a heartfelt greeting? Are the facilities clean and well maintained? Cleanliness should be a top priority, but don't be fooled by

FAMILY-FRIENDLY TIP

Preparing Your Child for a Vet Visit

One of the best ways to include your child in your Rottweiler's health care is to allow her to attend your dog's veterinary checkups. Remember, though, that it can be scary for a young child to visit a veterinary hospital for the first time. To make things easier on both your dog and your child (remember, anxiety can be contagious), prepare your child for the checkup before exam day arrives. Ask what she thinks might happen when your Rottie visits the vet. Discuss the differences between her doctor and a veterinarian. Tell your child that, just as she doesn't like having shots, your dog may flinch a bit when a needle goes in, but it will be over quickly— and that other tasks (such as getting weighed or having one's temperature taken) don't hurt a bit. An especially good veterinarian will explain the things she does to both you and your child so that keeping your Rottweiler healthy can be a family affair.

53

Feeling Good

fancy equipment and a well-decorated waiting room. These do not necessarily mean that the care is any better than that offered by a smaller, older veterinary hospital in your area.

Interview the Vet

When it is time for your appointment, make sure that you will be able to speak with the veterinarian one on one. A tour of the facilities is great, but it won't tell you a thing about the person who will ultimately be your partner in your dog's future health care. Ideally, you should like this person, but do realize that the most important thing is her ability to care for your Rottie. Some people don't interview well with owners but are great with the pets, so be sure to bring your dog along for this trip. He can offer you the best insight into whether this is the place for him.

Ask whether your dog will be able to see this same doctor each time he visits the hospital. With the exception of occasional business trips and vacations that make the doctor temporarily unavailable, your Rottie will likely do best if he can see the same vet consistently. Also, ask about the veterinarian's specialties. For example, does she offer ophthalmologic care? Complementary medicine? Does the hospital handle surgical procedures or refer them elsewhere? One very important piece of information is whether a caregiver is available to check on surgical patients spending the night at the hospital.

Find an After-Hours Clinic

In the event of an emergency, you should also know of the nearest after-

54

SENIOR DOG TIP

Coping With a Senior's Declining Health

Even a physically fit Rottweiler will likely confront at least some health problems as he ages, but you can meet these challenges by taking a proactive role in your senior dog's care. Dogs, like people, suffer from a slowing metabolism as they get older. The added weight that results from this leaves your pet more susceptible to heart and lung problems, joint problems, and problems with anesthesia. To be blunt, heavier dogs live shorter lives, so just managing your Rottie's weight tilts the odds in his favor.

Reacting quickly to any specific issues that may arise will also increase your dog's chances of keeping these problems minor ones. Even better than this, though, is preventing illness and injury in the first place. Your older dog is capable of many of the same things he did as a youngster, but his activities will now require a bit more planning and precaution. By facing this new phase of his life with love and respect, you can continue to enjoy time with your pet as he moves from vibrant adult to a vivacious, albeit slightly slowing, senior.

hours veterinary clinic. These facilities, which are typically open when traditional practices are closed, exist in most cities. You will pay more for treatment, of course, but these hospitals can be true lifesavers if your dog ever needs to see a veterinarian when his own vet has gone home for the day.

Annual Vet Visit

Once your Rottweiler puppy has been seen for an initial checkup and has completed his necessary vaccinations, he then only needs a regular examination once a year. When he is young, you may be tempted to put off this routine appointment. After all, if he is healthy, there's no need to rush to schedule the appointment at that annual date, right? Well, let me ask you this: How do you know that your dog is healthy? And even more important, do you want to keep him that way?

Dogs can be some of the most resilient creatures on earth. Whether they are hiding their symptoms or just being brave, the result is still the same. An undiagnosed illness will inevitably have more serious repercussions on your dog than a problem that is identified early and treated promptly. By simply feeling your dog's body, your veterinarian can detect irregularities, such as enlarged organs, which can signal disease. By looking in your dog's mouth, your vet may be able to tell you if your dog is anemic. (A lack of pink or reddish color can indicate this.) Your

vet may even be able to alert you to an imminent problem by comparing your dog's condition from one year to the next and helping him to avoid the situation, or at the least making it as easy to manage as possible.

During a typical checkup, your vet will weigh your dog, give him a thorough physical examination, and talk to you about any changes in his health since your last visit. Some vets recommend running routine blood work as your dog gets older and even increasing the frequency of routine exams from once to twice a year. Any necessary vaccinations will also be given at this time.

Vaccinations

At one time, being a responsible pet owner meant bringing your dog to his vet for all available vaccinations every year. Now, with growing scrutiny over

Vaccinations

Dogs are commonly vaccinated against all or some of the following:
- bordetella
- coronavirus
- distemper
- hepatitis
- leptospirosis
- Lyme disease
- parainfluenza
- parvovirus
- rabies

Vaccinations help protect dogs against various diseases.

not only the vaccinations themselves, but also the frequency at which they are administered, more and more owners are more selective about their dogs' vaccination schedules.

The most important thing to know is that vaccinations were developed for good reasons. Diseases such as rabies and parvovirus once wiped out entire kennels when they struck, so not vaccinating for these afflictions isn't the answer. At the same time, learning as much as we can about the current protocol—and adjusting our plans accordingly—can help ensure that our dogs are being protected against both the diseases themselves and any unnecessary side effects from the shots. The rabies vaccine, for instance, was once a yearly requirement but now

only needs to be administered every two or three years in most states. Other vaccines are currently being evaluated in this same way. Most other vaccines, however, are not required by law and may not be advisable for your Rottweiler unless he falls within a specific risk group for the illness. If you live in a warmer climate, for example, the vaccination for Lyme disease may likely be a smart move for your pet (I live in the suburbs, and my own dog tested positive for Lyme just recently), but if your dog only rarely visits public places, the bordetella (kennel cough) vaccine might not. Other factors to consider when planning your dog's vaccination schedule are your Rottie's age, general health, and reaction history to previous inoculations.

Talk to your veterinarian about what vaccines are necessary for your Rottweiler.

Parasites

Any organism that invades or attaches to another living thing and derives its nutrients from that animal's body is termed a parasite. Many owners instantly think of worms when they think of parasites, but fleas, mites, and ticks are also common parasites that can threaten a dog's health.

Internal Parasites

The internal varieties are quite possibly the most insidious of all parasites. Because they exist inside a dog's body, their presence is rarely obvious until they have begun to cause a problem. More generally referred to as worms, these organisms can range from a 4-inch (10.2-cm) roundworm to a 14-inch (35.6-cm) heartworm.

The following are some common internal parasites:

- heartworms
- hookworms
- houndworms
- whipworms

External Parasites

External parasites exist on the exterior of a dog's body. Although they are easier to spot than the internal variety, these pests can be just as dangerous as internal parasites. Because most survive off the blood of the host animal, they can easily cause internal problems by attaching themselves to your pet.

Fleas

Although not usually thought of as a dangerous problem, flea bites can lead to a number of serious canine health problems. By protecting your dog with a monthly flea preventive, you can easily avoid a painful and exasperating infestation and possibly several other health issues. Prevention is considerably easier than treatment, but if your dog is already serving as a breeding ground, don't despair. If you are committed to victory, you can win the battle by thoroughly treating both your dog and your home. A wide variety of products on the market are available to accomplish this goal, from conventional shampoos and sprays to natural alternatives that are more pet and environment-friendly. Talk to your veterinarian to see which ones are best for your dog's situation.

Mites

Mites are extremely small arachnids—so small, in fact, that they can only be seen with considerable magnification. Although you have probably never heard of the various types of mites that affect dogs—cheyletiella, demodex, and sarcoptes—you have surely heard of mange, the skin disease caused by many species. Like fleas, mites cause itching and inflammation and can sometimes be passed to humans. Unlike fleas, though, mites are not currently treated in a proactive way. Instead, a dog is only medicated once a mite problem has been positively identified. Typically, this includes the use of a topical or injectable insecticide, but owners may also have to treat their homes.

Ticks

Ticks are also arachnids, but the size of different species varies considerably. This makes it extremely important for owners to always be on the lookout for these treacherous creatures. Armed with a natural anesthetic that prevents animals from feeling their bites, ticks can attach themselves quite firmly to a dog (or human) before ever being noticed.

If you find a tick on your Rottweiler, how you remove it is just

SENIOR DOG TIP

Senior Schedule

Your aging Rottweiler should have a routine exam every six months instead of just once a year. By identifying any existing afflictions before they become more serious, you increase your dog's chances of beating them.

as important as removing it in the first place. Because ticks can transmit certain diseases to humans, the first thing you should do is don a pair of latex gloves. Next, locate the tick, and with a pair of fine-pointed tweezers, grasp and pull it gently and slowly from your dog's skin. Be careful not to pinch your dog, but do get as close to his skin as you can. Also, be very careful to pull the tick straight out. Pulling too quickly or twisting can cause the tick's body to separate from its head, which can remain imbedded in your pet and leave him vulnerable to infection. (If this happens, contact your veterinarian for further instruction.)

Once the tick is out, drop it into some isopropyl alcohol to kill it. Never use your bare hands or feet to kill a tick, because any infection could then pass to you. As soon as the tick has been properly disposed of, clean the bite wound with disinfectant, and sterilize your tweezers with some fresh alcohol.

Ticks vary in size and color, but the longer one has been attached to your Rottie, the bigger it will be. Some can even engorge to the size of a grape. Remember, though, that when it comes to ticks, size doesn't matter. The smallest of them all, the deer tick (which causes Lyme disease), can be the deadliest. For this reason, it is best that you follow up with your Rottweiler's veterinarian whenever you remove a tick from your dog.

Inspect your Rottie for fleas and ticks after he has been playing outdoors.

Breed-Specific Illnesses

Some breeds are more susceptible to particular illnesses than others. And while Rottweilers certainly don't top the list of illness-prone dogs, they do have their share of common maladies. Although some of these afflictions can be serious, most are fortunately manageable.

Epilepsy

Epilepsy is a disorder of the nervous system that causes convulsions, ranging from mild (petit mal) to severe (grand mal) in nature. Few things are as scary as watching your dog endure an epileptic seizure. Unfortunately, I know firsthand how frightening this can be, because my dog Molly suffers from idiopathic epilepsy, meaning no identifiable cause can be found for her seizures.

Symptoms

It is impossible to accurately describe what will happen if your Rottweiler ever seizes, because every dog (and in some cases, every episode) is a little different. Molly's seizures usually begin with her shaking, a common symptom, but she also usually drools excessively, loses control of her bladder and bowels, and appears to

be temporarily paralyzed during the episode. Dogs may also act anxious, stumble, or make running movements with their legs. They will not, however, swallow their tongues. Most seizures last from one to three minutes. Episodes lasting longer than five minutes could indicate that a grand mal seizure is taking place, so seek veterinary care immediately if the symptoms do not subside after this period.

The most important thing to remember if your dog does seize is to remain as calm as possible. As difficult as this may be, I cannot stress its importance enough. By overreacting, you can unintentionally prolong the seizure or overlook an important detail about it.

Treatment

Unfortunately, no test can diagnose idiopathic epilepsy, but by ruling out other common causes of seizures, your vet can narrow the list of what might be triggering your Rottie's problem. Some common causes include hypothyroidism, Lyme disease, and tumors.

Once you and your vet have narrowed the diagnosis, you will then have to decide on a treatment plan. Medication may not be necessary if your dog's seizures are infrequent (occurring only a few times a year, for instance). If they increase in frequency or intensity, however, you

A Makeshift Muzzle

If your dog is ever seriously hurt, you must exercise caution when touching him. Although your dog may never hurt you intentionally, if he is in extreme pain or disoriented as a result of his injury, he is much more likely to lash out at anyone who approaches him—even someone he loves.

If you own a muzzle, this is an excellent time to use it. If you don't, you can make an impromptu version from rolled gauze. Being careful not to pull the fur around his face, wrap a length of gauze around your dog's own muzzle several times, and tie it securely under his chin. Then, tie the ends at the back of the head near the top of the neck. This will not prevent your dog from breathing, but it can protect you from a nasty bite. He may try to get it off, though, so remain vigilant as you seek the help of a veterinarian.

may need to consider placing your dog on an anticonvulsant medication. Changes in diet, vaccinations, and environment may also have an effect on your dog's susceptibility to an epileptic episode.

Hip Dysplasia

A common problem in Rottweilers and other larger breeds, hip dysplasia occurs when the hip joint is not properly formed. This may result from a genetic predisposition or from environmental factors. Because the average age of onset is two years (the problem is nearly impossible to diagnose in dogs younger than six months old), it is extremely important that owners ask potential breeders for documentation that a puppy's parents and grandparents have been screened for the disease. Responsible breeders should only be breeding dogs who have received official clearance from the Orthopedic Foundation for Animals (OFA). Because the condition is not always genetic, however, even the most careful selection of a breeder cannot guarantee that your Rottweiler will not develop hip dysplasia.

Symptoms

The most common symptom of hip dysplasia is pain or discomfort, especially first thing in the morning or directly following exercise. If you notice your dog limping or avoiding activity, it may be time to have him checked. By seeking treatment early, you will likely be able to relieve your pet's pain, return him to greater mobility, and prevent the unnecessary loss of muscle tone.

Treatment

Once an X-ray confirms the diagnosis, a treatment plan must be chosen. In more serious cases, surgery may be necessary. Sometimes, though, owners can improve their dogs' prognosis by making smaller changes. If your dog is too heavy, reducing weight is a great place to start. Additionally, exercise that focuses on range of motion and muscle building can be extremely helpful, provided it limits stress on your dog's joints. Ensuring that your Rottie has warm, comfortable sleeping quarters, utilizing massage and physical

If your dog appears unusually listless or lethargic, a trip to the vet is in order.

therapy, and taking simple steps to make your dog's everyday activities less painful can also be beneficial.

Prevention

The best way to help your Rottie avoid hip dysplasia is to provide him with a sensible fitness plan. Overweight dogs are particularly prone to dysplasia, so overfeeding can increase your pet's risk. And although exercise should be part of virtually any dog's routine, overexercising can also expose your Rottweiler to this problem (especially in younger dogs), so make sure that your dog isn't overdoing it, either. Injuries can also increase the incidence of hip dysplasia.

Gastric Dilatation-Volvulus

Considered a medical emergency, gastric dilatation-volvulus (GDV) (also known as bloat) is a condition caused by the distension of the stomach, usually with swallowed air. The cause is unknown, but an anatomic predisposition may exist. Deep-chested dogs like the Rottweiler are most commonly affected. Overeating may also increase an individual's chances of suffering from this condition, as can exercising either directly before or after eating. Many veterinarians think that eating and drinking from dishes held in a raised table can also contribute to a dog's likelihood of experiencing this very serious problem.

Symptoms

The signs of GDV can be obscure, but if the condition is not diagnosed quickly enough, it can be

Does Your Rottweiler Need Health Insurance?

Although the scale is smaller, the cost of canine health care is rising, just like the price of our own medical care. In addition to annual vet visits, dog owners should anticipate having their pets neutered, providing them with regular medications for heartworm and flea and tick prevention, and heading to the vet's office for occasional unexpected problems that may arise. These costs can add up quickly.

A great way to be sure that these costs remain manageable is to purchase health insurance for your Rottweiler. Several national companies offer such policies that reimburse owners for everything from annual visits to prescriptions. Is it worth it? The answer is also much like that of your own health insurance premiums. As long as your dog is healthy, this protection may seem like a luxury, but if he ever suffers from a catastrophic illness or injury, it could make all the difference. If you are interested in purchasing pet health insurance, ask your vet to recommend a provider.

lethal, killing a dog within 6 to 12 hours. This makes it imperative that diagnosis be made as soon as possible. A dog suffering from bloat typically writhes around, struggling to belch or even breathe.

Treatment

A vet may insert a tube into the stomach to relieve the built-up gas, but depending on the severity of the situation, this may not be possible. In more drastic cases, surgery is necessary.

Heart Disease

Heart problems can be genetic, but they can also have external causes. Many of these are the same for dogs as they are for people—mainly a diet too high in fat and an insufficient exercise routine. By now you may be tiring of hearing about the importance of a healthy eating and exercise plan for your pet, but it truly is one of the best ways to ward off all kinds of dangerous afflictions. Many different forms of heart disease exist, but most can be avoided or managed with this simple, common-sense approach.

Symptoms

Because symptoms are not always obvious until a problem has intensified, it is extremely important that owners take steps to keep their dogs' hearts

The proper amount of exercise helps your Rottie live a longer, healthier life.

healthy before one develops. Early signs that your dog may be experiencing cardio-vascular issues include coughing and struggling to breathe (relatively easy for an owner to spot) and an enlarged heart (something a veterinarian may be able to identify during a simple physical exam).

Treatment

Treatments may range from nutritional therapy to surgery.

Hypothyroidism

Hypothyroidism is a condition in which the thyroid gland doesn't secrete a sufficient amount of thyroid hormone. Because the thyroid (two butterfly-shaped lobes located at the back of the neck) helps manage your dog's metabolism (his ability to utilize

Facts and Myths About Neutering

One of the best things you can do for your Rottweiler is have him or her neutered (males are castrated, and females are spayed) as soon as possible. Sterilizing pets helps them live longer, healthier lives. Castrating males eliminates the threat of testicular cancer, and it also reduces the risk of prostate cancer. Spaying your female Rottie will prevent her from suffering from ovarian or uterine cancers, and it will significantly lessen her risk of breast cancer, especially if she is spayed before her first heat cycle.

Still, the myths persist, which is why it's so important to know the facts from the fiction:

MYTH: I don't want my male dog to feel like less of a male.
FACT: Pets don't have any concept of sexual identity or ego. Neutering will not change a pet's basic personality. He doesn't suffer any kind of emotional reaction or identity crisis when neutered.

MYTH: But my dog is so special, I want a puppy just like her.
FACT: A dog may be a great pet, but that doesn't mean her offspring will be a carbon copy. Professional animal breeders who follow generations of bloodlines can't guarantee they will get just what they want out of a particular litter. A pet owner's chances are even slimmer. In fact, an entire litter of puppies might receive all of a pet's (and her mate's) worst characteristics.

MYTH: It's too expensive to have my pet neutered.
FACT: The cost of neutering depends on the sex, size, and age of the pet, your veterinarian's fees, and a number of other variables. But whatever the actual price, sterilization is a one-time cost—a relatively small cost when compared to all the benefits. Most important, it's a very small price to pay for the health of your pet and the prevention of the births of more unwanted pets.

(Courtesy of the HSUS)

the nutrients he consumes), an underactive thyroid can cause your dog to gain weight at an alarming rate for no apparent reason.

Like epilepsy, hypothyroidism can be difficult to identify, but unlike the former condition, this one can be definitively diagnosed once the right test is performed. Because the symptoms are so varied, though, your veterinarian might not lean in the direction of hypothyroidism until a thorough history is taken and a complete physical examination is performed.

Symptoms

Just a few of the other signs of this condition are behavior changes, skin problems, hair loss, chronic ear infections, and intolerance to the cold. As stated previously, a dog suffering from hypothyroidism can even experience seizures.

Treatment

Once a diagnosis is made through a blood test, your dog can then be treated with a synthetic hormone. This is usually highly effective. While your dog will need to be seen for routine checkups to ensure proper dosage, he will likely live a long and healthy life with no further symptoms of this illness.

Von Willebrand's Disease

Similar to hemophilia, von Willebrand's disease (VWD) is a genetic bleeding disorder.

Symptoms

Symptoms include excessive or prolonged bleeding. A dog may suffer symptoms as mild as a toenail that will take a little extra time to clot to more serious hemorrhaging following an injury or surgical procedure.

Treatment

The disease can be avoided through the careful selection of breeding stock, but blood tests are necessary, because dogs may be carriers without ever showing any symptoms. Currently, no cure or effective treatment is available for VWD, so keeping an affected dog away from potential dangers (ranging from sharp rocks outdoors to furniture with pointed edges indoors) is of the utmost importance.

General Illnesses

In addition to the breed-specific illnesses that your Rottweiler may face, several other ailments commonly affect dogs in general. This doesn't mean that all dogs will suffer from these conditions at some point in their lives or even that your dog's case will be severe if he is afflicted. Still, knowledge is the best defense if your dog is faced with any of the following situations.

Allergies

It is estimated that 20 percent of dogs in the United States harbor some type of allergy. Like humans, dogs can be allergic to virtually anything, but food is the culprit in many cases—particularly dairy products, wheat, and corn.

Symptoms

We humans tend to think of allergies in

terms of sneezing, watery eyes, and itching. For our dogs, though, it is primarily the last of these three symptoms—itching—that indicates an allergic reaction.

Treatment

If you suspect that your dog is suffering from an allergy, ask your veterinarian about placing him on a hypoallergenic diet. Although allergy tests are available for dogs, they tend to be rather expensive and not

extremely accurate. The better method of identifying the allergen is to combine the specialized diet with good old-fashioned trial and error. Once your dog has been eating the new food exclusively for several weeks (and shown no signs of a problem), you may then start adding other foods back into his regimen one at a time.

Cancer

It's a word that no one likes to hear, yet cancer is one of the most common diseases that pets face today. When diagnosed early, our dogs have a significantly higher chance of winning a battle against this brutal illness.

Symptoms

One of the most common symptoms of cancer include lumps or bumps found on the dog. Many times these abnormalities are benign, but they can sometimes signal a malignancy, so leave no area unchecked. Baylie, a dog belonging to a friend of mine, once developed a cancerous tumor on her genitals. If my friend hadn't examined her thoroughly, this life-threatening growth may have been missed until it was too late.

Prevention

One of the best ways to prevent cancer from striking your dog is to sterilize him or her at a young age. Other factors that can have a tremendous impact on an animal's likelihood of developing certain cancers include a dog's diet, exercise plan, and environment. Even the chemicals within our homes (from cleaning agents to insecticides) may be affecting our dogs, so limiting (or eliminating) the use of toxic substances is always a smart step.

Treatment

A variety of treatment options are available, including radiation, chemotherapy, and surgery, so if your dog has been diagnosed with cancer, don't despair. This is another canine illness with which I unfortunately have personal experience, and I can tell you that cancer is not always terminal. My own dog, Jonathan, had a mast cell tumor successfully removed after I discovered it one day while grooming him. My friend's dog, Baylie, is alive and kicking after having not just one but two separate mast cell tumors removed. Owners must act quickly, though. One of Baylie's tumors grew from the size of a blueberry to the size of a marble in just one week. Her early diagnosis undoubtedly saved her life.

Inspect your Rottie's eyes regularly; if they seem to be irritated or infected, take him to the vet immediately.

Ear Infections

Ear infections are relatively common in dogs, but with proper treatment and sensible precautions, they don't have to be a recurrent problem.

Symptoms

If your Rottie is suffering from an ear infection, it will be hard to miss the signs. Your dog will likely shake his head or scratch at his ears uncontrollably in response to the discomfort. Tilting of the head in one direction is also a sign of an ear infection. The ear itself may appear red or swollen, with or without a black or yellowish discharge. Often a strong, offensive odor emanates from the infected ear.

Treatment

At the first sign of an ear infection, bring your dog to the veterinarian for an examination. The vet will need to make sure that the eardrum is not ruptured before prescribing a medication, because some drugs can lead to hearing loss if this is the case.

Once a diagnosis has been made, your vet will probably prescribe an antibiotic to clear up the infection. A middle ear infection can take up to several weeks to resolve completely, but most cases of otitis externa (an infection of the external ear canal) improve relatively quickly once treatment has begun. An ear infection is not a problem that will go away on its own; veterinary treatment must be sought.

Eye Infections

Common eye infections such as conjunctivitis (commonly called pink eye because of the condition's primary symptom) or keratoconjunctivitis (also called dry eye) can lead to more serious eye problems if left untreated. For this important reason, you should check your Rottweiler's eyes regularly. An infection may result from an injury to the eye or from the bacteria that your dog encounters on a daily basis.

Symptoms

If your dog is suffering from an eye infection, he may experience discomfort and respond by pawing at the eye, risking additional injury. If you notice any redness or discharge from your dog's eyes, consult your veterinarian.

Treatment

Most often, an antibiotic ointment is all that is necessary to clear up the problem.

Alternative Therapies

Alternative medicine includes a group of traditional treatments such as acupuncture, flower essences, and homeopathy. At one time, people sought alternative treatments when all other options had been exhausted. Today, however, traditional medicine is increasingly utilized alongside more conventional techniques in treating a full range of health problems.

Acupuncture

Acupuncture, a procedure involving the insertion of needles into specific body parts (not always where the problem exists), can be surprisingly effective. Again, I speak from experience, as one of my own dogs was once treated with acupuncture. This method healed my dog's torn anterior cruciate ligament (ACL) and prevented costly surgery with a two- to three-month recovery period. Other conditions for which acupuncture may be useful include cardiovascular disorders, chronic respiratory conditions, and gastrointestinal problems.

Flower Essences

One form of alternative medicine that can be easily administered at home (with a certain amount of prior knowledge, of course) is the use of flower essences. Developed in the 1930s by Dr. Edward Bach, the practice of using these innocuous ingredients to strengthen your dog's immunity poses virtually no risk to your pet but can help him prevent numerous health problems. The underlying philosophy of this method, which involves infusing flowers and other

plants in spring water, is that creating emotional balance can help fight illness and foster healing. If you think that flower essences may be useful to your pet, ask your vet to recommend a particular essence or book on the topic. Because flower essences are typically administered just a drop or two at a time, remember to pick up a plastic eye dropper for your Rottie, as a glass instrument may break and injure your pet.

Homeopathy

Homeopathy involves treating a disease with infinitesimal doses of drugs that in massive amounts actually cause the disease symptoms that your dog is battling. While this may sound counterproductive, it is important to note that this is the very premise on which modern vaccines are based. By introducing only a minute amount of the offending agent, your dog's body is able to create an immunity against it that will subsequently react in force to the real threat.

Even if you know a great deal about homeopathy, this is one treatment that should never be dabbled in or treated lightly. Because precise dosing is a must—and smaller doses can be even more powerful than larger ones with this modality—it is vital that only a

The Expert Knows

Finding an Alternative Caregiver

To find a licensed canine acupuncturist or homeopathic caregiver in your area, contact the American Academy of Veterinary Acupuncture (AAVA) at www.aava.org or the Academy of Veterinary Homeopathy (AVH) at www.theavh.org.

trained professional be allowed to treat your dog with homeopathy.

Good canine health is about so much more than fighting illnesses and nursing injuries. It is about taking a proactive approach, too. A healthy diet, regular exercise, and even time set aside for relaxing with his owner can have an enormous effect on your dog's physical and mental health. As you spend more and more time with your Rottweiler, you will notice things about him that others—even professional caregivers—may miss. Pay attention as this instinct develops, because it may be the quickest route to preventing or solving a health problem.

Feeling Good

Chapter 6

Being Good

All dogs must be trained, but with larger breeds such as the Rottweiler, the need is even more time sensitive, because your Rottie puppy will reach a formidable size within just months of joining your household. If he isn't taught how to behave properly while he is young and relatively small, training will only be more difficult down the road.

I t is also important that your Rottweiler receive the training he needs so that he isn't targeted by individuals who subscribe to the stereotype that Rottweilers are naturally dangerous. It is far more difficult to complain about a dog who behaves properly. Some might still try, of course, but their cynicism won't get them very far in the face of a dog who sits, heels, and stays on command.

Socialization

Socializing a dog consists of exposing him regularly to a variety of people and animals in an effort to teach him proper behavior around others. Rottweilers aren't any more difficult to socialize than other dogs, but the urgency is greater with Rotties than with most smaller, less intimidating breeds.

How to Socialize Your Rottie

Begin exposing your dog to as many people as possible as soon as you bring him home. Invite friends and family to visit so that they can meet your new puppy, take him with you whenever you run a pet-friendly errand, and be sure to include children and fellow animals in the mix.

Even strangers who might be uncomfortable with a full-grown Rottweiler will likely be drawn to a Rottie puppy. This paves the way for your dog to grow into a friendly adult who exudes an affable nature and may even win over similarly hesitant humans later in life. You can make the interaction an even more pleasant one

Your Rottie should be well socialized to a variety of different things, including other dogs.

by carrying tasty treats with you wherever you and your dog go and allowing anyone who wants to pet your pup the chance to offer him a treat as well. This helps your dog associate people with positive things.

Ideally, your dog should be exposed to people each day. As your Rottie gets bigger, take care to ensure the safety of everyone he encounters. This includes other animals and small children who can easily be knocked down by an enthusiastic puppy who doesn't yet know his own size and strength. For this reason also, training should begin as early as possible. Everyone will be more open to socializing with your pet if he shows good manners, like not jumping up or barking incessantly. This doesn't mean that your Rottie can't play with smaller dogs or kids, though; he must simply learn to be gentle with them.

All dog owners must respect the wishes of those who do not want to join in the fun of canine socialization. The best rule to follow when you are looking for people to interact with your Rottweiler is to ask before allowing your dog to approach them.

Better yet, wait to see if they approach you first. You may be surprised by how many people do, but some people simply don't like dogs.

The Expert Knows

Finding a Trainer

If you are new to dog training, consider enlisting the help of a professional. Whether you prefer the camaraderie of a class or the personal attention of an individual trainer, learning the basics from a pro can help lay an ideal foundation for your Rottweiler's future learning.

Remember, animals can sense these things, so what your dog gains from this stressful exchange will be limited at best.

Crate Training

For many Rottweiler owners, the idea of not having a crate for their pets seems unimaginable. This versatile enclosure can function as a safe place to keep your dog when you cannot properly supervise him, a convenient spot to feed him (especially if you have other pets), and a home away from home while traveling with your Rottie. It may also serve as an effective housetraining tool.

The most important thing to remember about the crate is that it should never be used as punishment. This doesn't mean that you can't place your

Being Good

Rottweiler puppy in his crate while you clean a soiled carpet or when a non-dog lover visits your home, but be careful not to admonish your dog while doing so, because this can lead him to attach negative feelings to his crate.

Never leave your Rottie in the crate for longer than necessary, and keep in mind that no dog should ever be crated for more than six hours.

How to Crate Train Your Rottie

When you first introduce the crate, refrain from closing the door at all. Leave it open, and allow your dog to investigate it on his own. If he doesn't, tempt him by placing a favorite toy or treat inside it. Praise him for entering the crate (even if he only stays inside for a moment or two), and offer a second reward as added reinforcement. Once he seems comfortable with spending time in the crate, try closing the door for short periods—only a minute or two initially. Again, praise your dog's tolerance, and

The versatile crate functions as a safe place to temporarily keep your dog when you are unable to supervise him.

always try to end on a positive note. Pushing your Rottweiler to accept the crate too quickly can cause him to resist it even more intensely, so be patient. Given a little time, your dog will likely see his kennel as a special place of his own, and you will probably find him in it even when he doesn't have to be there.

Whenever your dog will be in his crate for more than an hour, give him the opportunity to relieve himself before entering and once again when he is released. You should never leave a dog in a crate all day. If you cannot make it back home after a few hours, ask a friend or neighbor to stop by to provide your dog with a chance to empty his bladder or bowels and to stretch his legs some before heading back inside the enclosure. If this isn't possible, and your dog cannot be trusted alone in your home, consider employing a dog daycare service while you work or are otherwise engaged. A dog left cooped up in his crate all day every day will likely start acting out in an attempt to show his displeasure with this arrangement.

Crate Alternatives

Even with all its advantages, the crate is not for every dog—or every owner. If you don't feel comfortable using a crate, there is no reason that you must. Likewise, if your dog seems particularly resistant to the concept, other solutions are available. A pet or baby gate, for example, can keep your dog contained to a pet-proofed room while you are away or when you need to clean up a housetraining accident. It can also help you separate your pets at mealtimes. Traveling is the only instance in which you may truly need a crate, but even this may be worked around as long as you won't be flying. Many vehicles can be equipped with pet guards that keep animals contained to a certain area while riding.

Housetraining

Everyone loves the idea of getting a new puppy—until it's time for housetraining, that is. All your family members will be there to welcome your new Rottweiler puppy home, but watch how fast they disappear when it's time to clean up the first housetraining mistake. Take heart, though. The job of teaching your dog the appropriate places to eliminate isn't nearly as difficult as it may seem to most people. Even the job of cleaning up accidents can be done quickly and efficiently once an owner knows a few essential tricks.

The Importance of Positive Training

Psychologists have long known that positive reinforcement is a far more effective teaching tool than punishment, but there exists one even more important reason to use positive training methods: They help you to build a more positive relationship with your dog. Heading out to socialize your Rottie with a quick walk to the park? Bring along some treats for strangers to offer him. This helps him form a positive association with meeting new people. When he eliminates in the proper spot outdoors, praise him enthusiastically. It is the best way to ensure a repeat performance. He instantly sees you as his greatest supporter and strives to please you as you teach him more and more new things.

How to Housetrain Your Rottie

The best thing about housetraining is that you can begin this important task as soon as you bring your Rottie home. If you're lucky, your breeder has given you a great head start by providing the entire young litter of puppies with newspapers inside the home and by taking the pups outdoors regularly as they get a bit older. I often brag that when my husband and I went to visit our dog Molly at just a few weeks old, she readily left the room to eliminate on her paper in the middle of our play session. While our breeder didn't focus her efforts on housetraining, she did praise Molly for this and merely redirected her whenever she eliminated in an inappropriate spot. This is the basic foundation for successful housetraining. Praise your dog whenever he eliminates where he should, and simply redirect him when he misses this target. Refrain from punishing him. In addition to not helping your situation, it could actually hurt your chances of future success. (More on this later.)

Whenever your dog goes in the correct spot, praise him like crazy. You may even use an edible reward intermittently if you wish. A great trick for teaching your dog to go on command is telling him to go pee or poop (or whatever words you choose for these activities) as soon as your dog begins eliminating. This will help him to understand the meaning of the words and know what you want him to do next time when you take him outside and instruct him this way.

The best tool at your disposal during housetraining is your clock. Watch it like a hawk, and bring your

Are You Listening?

In recent years, dog owners have become impressively adept at interpreting canine body language. I myself watch my dogs' tails whenever they get into a scuffle to see if they really mean business, or as is the case most often, they're just playing. (An arched back with a tail held high is a sign of aggression, but wagging indicates just the opposite.) What about the other things our dogs do to communicate with us, though? Are we really listening when our dogs speak?

Say your dog barks at you repeatedly in short bursts and in a particularly high-pitched tone. Well, he probably either needs to relieve himself, or he merely wants to play with you. Head outdoors so he can do both. What if your dog barks only once or twice in a lower, deeper voice? Most likely he is announcing a stranger or alerting you to something else. If your dog whines or yelps, however, he is indicating stress or pain, so check him over to see what might be causing his discomfort. The very premise of training is to successfully communicate our expectations to our dogs, but it is a good idea to listen to what our dogs are telling us as well. Communication, after all, is a two-way street.

Rottweiler puppy to his potty spot every two hours in the very beginning. As your dog gets just a bit older, you can lengthen this interval accordingly. A three-month old puppy only needs to be taken out every three hours, and a four-month-old should only need to go every four hours. An adult Rottie should be able to hold his bladder for up to eight hours, but try not to make him wait more than four to six. By sticking to a schedule for both eating and eliminating, you help your dog fall into a routine.

Praise your dog when he eliminates in the proper spot.

Some owners like to teach their dogs to ask when they have to eliminate. If you share this goal, consider attaching a noisemaker of some sort on or near your door. This item must be placed low enough for your dog to reach, and you should begin using it immediately by sounding it off each and every time you take your dog outside to eliminate. Many dogs simply go to the door and bark or fuss when they need to do their business. This too can be taught by barking yourself before heading out the door. Although you may find it comical to do this, you will thank yourself later when your dog alerts you of his needs, thus avoiding an unnecessary mess.

Punishment

Punishment sends an ineffective and confusing message to a dog. You may have just found the unpleasant package left on your living room carpet by your Rottweiler, but even minutes after the deed has been done, your dog may no longer understand why you are angry with him. In some cases, punishing him can even leave him with the misconception that something is bad about relieving himself, a concept that can ultimately lead to health problems if your dog tries to hold his bladder or bowels out of fear of being punished. Whatever you do, never resort to physical punishment. A dog learns nothing from being hit with a newspaper (or someone's hand) or having his nose rubbed in excrement.

Housetraining Accidents

You will not be cleaning up daily accidents forever. By cleaning them right the first time, though, you can help your dog along in the housetraining process. You see, a dog will prefer to eliminate in a spot he has used previously. This is why it's vital to remove any signs from the area that may attract your Rottie in the future. Always begin by completely absorbing the wetness from the area you're cleaning. Even small amounts left behind will inspire a repeat offense. Only after you get every drop out of your carpet should you then wash the area. Several products are made especially for further absorbing any odor left behind. Many owners have found these to be extremely effective in discouraging their dogs from revisiting a particular spot. Because urine contains a high percentage of ammonia, avoid this ingredient in any cleaning product. Ideally, pet-friendly products are a better option even when doing routine cleaning throughout your home.

Basic Commands

To some people, basic training sounds more like boot camp than a fun canine pastime, but training your dog to perform a handful of simple commands can be fun as well as practical. Even after your dog has mastered the commands, you will continue to enjoy the benefits of this time well spent. The feeling will also be contagious, because a well-mannered dog is a welcome guest in all dog-friendly places.

Sit

I recommend teaching the *sit* command before any others because it is truly a hands-on experience for owners and tends to be an easily mastered task for most dogs. A dog who obeys the *sit* command can be interrupted if he begins to do something unpleasant, such as jumping

FAMILY-FRIENDLY TIP

Teach Your Children

If you plan to participate in a formal dog training class with your Rottie, ask if multiple family members are allowed to attend the sessions. Many trainers welcome family involvement, because the more support your dog receives, the quicker he learns. Particularly with children, though, it is essential that everyone involved understands the importance of consistency. For younger kids, this means teaching them a simple training technique for a specific command (most kids love teaching the *sit* command) and having them practice it repeatedly with your pet. This helps keep everyone focused on the task at hand and stacks the odds for training success in your Rottweiler's favor.

on company, when he is instructed to sit. This also provides an excellent foundation for all future commands.

How to Teach Sit

To teach this command, simply hold a treat up over your dog's nose and slowly move it back over his head as you issue the *sit* command. Most dogs will naturally move into the sitting position. Next, give him the treat, but don't forget to utter an enthusiastic "Good boy!" Although edible rewards can be extremely effective for training, they cannot replace the power of praise.

Come

I am a huge advocate of teaching dogs the *come* command, because teaching this one word can literally save your dog's life. If your Rottie ever gets away from you, having successfully taught this single command is like having an invisible leash at your disposal.

How to Teach Come

The best way to teach this command is to catch your dog already in the act of coming to you. Whenever you see your Rottweiler moving your way, say "Come" in an upbeat tone, and praise him lavishly for doing so. Soon he will begin to associate the word with the action.

You can work with your dog in any

Basic training helps your Rottie behave appropriately in a variety of situations.

safe environment— a fenced backyard or a large, open family room, for example. You can also practice with your dog on an extendable leash nearly anywhere. If working off-lead, be sure to have a friend help you, because it is especially important that you have a way of making your dog comply with the command. Most important, never admonish your dog for coming when called—if he has done something unpleasant, for example. Your dog should never fear coming to you.

Stay

Like come, the *stay* command can possibly be an issue of life or death. If your Rottie is ever off his leash near a moving vehicle or a less-than-friendly fellow animal, you must know that you are able to trust him to stay put until you can reach him. If, like me, you are on the small side, this command also proves useful in everyday situations once your adult dog's size has made it nearly impossible for you to physically make him stay in one place.

The *stay* command is best taught once your dog has mastered sitting.

How to Teach Stay

After issuing the *sit* command, raise your hand and say "Stay" as you back up very slowly. In the beginning, your Rottie may only remain still for a few seconds, but it is especially important to offer praise during this time, however short. Be careful, though, because rewarding him just a moment too late will reinforce the wrong behavior.

Gradually increase the number of steps you take away from your dog. You should also increase the amount of time before you offer praise or a reward. Eventually, your dog should be able to stay for about a minute or longer with you at least 10 feet (3.0 m) away. In competitive obedience, this length of time must be even longer.

Down

Putting a dog into a sitting position has a way of lowering his overall excitement level. Likewise, the *down*

Keep It Simple

You may at first think that the bigger the reward, the harder your dog will work toward reaching your training goals. Although no one can deny the effectiveness of using edible rewards, this is one area where smaller rewards will likely work better than larger ones. Overly large biscuits or crunchy foods that require a lot of chewing will take extra time to consume and distract your Rottweiler from the task at hand.

Begin the training process by offering your dog individual pieces of kibble. If he doesn't seem inspired by these, change to a similarly sized dog treat or cubed chicken or cheese. Particularly in the case of the latter items, though, be sure to adjust your dog's meal portions so he doesn't gain unnecessary weight from being a good learner.

command takes this to an even more subdued point. A dog in a *down* position (in which the dog lies down on his belly) is more relaxed than one chomping at the bit.

How to Teach Down

Teaching the down command is most easily accomplished by using an edible reward. With your dog in a sitting position, issue the command while lowering the treat in front of him. Most dogs will naturally lower their bodies to get the treat, but if your Rottie does not, try slowly pulling the treat away from him. Eventually, you should start issuing the command before even bringing out the reward, because you do not want your dog's compliance to depend on the physical motion of lowering the treat.

Heel

Teaching your dog to heel essentially means showing him how to walk alongside you while you are walking and to sit patiently whenever you stop. The heel command is particularly useful if you take your Rottie for frequent walks on a leash or if you plan to involve him in formal obedience trials.

This is another command for which the *sit* command is a prerequisite.

How to Teach Heel

Begin by walking your dog on your left side with the leash in your right hand and a treat in your left. When you stop, say "Sit." When he complies, reward him and say "Heel." Begin

walking again, stopping periodically to practice this two-part exercise. Your ultimate goal is for your dog to comfortably walk alongside you, stopping whenever you do.

Drop It/Leave It

The *drop it* and *leave it* commands can protect your dog from any number of dangers, including choking and poisoning. *Drop it* can also be helpful when playing fetch.

The heel command teaches your Rottie to walk politely on leash.

SENIOR DOG TIP

The Adult Learner

The biggest difference between training a younger dog and an older dog is that, in the latter situation, much of the focus is remedial. Although a puppy has no deeply ingrained behaviors that must be corrected, an older dog in need of training has had some time to become more set in his unpleasant ways. Of course, it is far easier to create a new habit than reverse an old one, but it is possible. Persistence and patience are both fundamental here. Show your dog that you won't give up on him, and you will likely begin to see something he has never shown anyone else—an enthusiastic love for learning.

How to Teach Drop It

Using a favorite toy, encourage your dog to play with the item for a few minutes before you say "Drop it." As you issue the command, gently remove the toy from his mouth. Praise him immediately for complying, and return the item to him so that you can repeat this exercise. In the beginning, your Rottie may not be wild about relinquishing the item. With a little time and a lot of praise, though, he will comply without any physical prompting.

How to Teach Leave It

Although similar to the *drop it* command, the *leave it* command works a little differently, because you do not want your dog to touch the item in question in the first place. The best way to teach this command is to give your dog a favorite toy and encourage him to play with it. After a minute or so, toss another favorite item in his general direction. If, as you hope, his attention is captured by this toy, immediately say "Leave it" and use the leash to keep him from touching it. Again, eventually you won't need to physically prevent him from touching the second item, but for now, you merely want to interrupt his natural tendency to investigate the tossed toy. Once your dog shows success with this, you should then begin practicing the command when he is off leash.

Tricks

The fun thing about teaching your dog tricks is that there's virtually no limit to what you can teach him. The most important thing to know when teaching your Rottweiler a new trick is to be patient with him. If you are persistent, he will most likely learn whatever it is, but selecting a trick he has an affinity for always helps.

The following are a few tricks to try with your Rottie.

Shake Hands

The easiest way to teach your Rottweiler to shake hands is to begin with your dog in a sitting position. Take his paw into your hand as you gently lift and shake it, saying "Shake" or whatever phrase you choose. When you release his paw, he should lower it to the floor or ground. Reward your dog heartily for complying. After practicing this for a while, again command your dog to sit, but this time merely extend your hand as you say your catch phrase. Continue to repeat this exercise to reinforce the trick, and never forget to praise him for a job well done.

Roll Over

Before you can teach a dog to roll over, he should first learn the *down* command. This enables him to begin in the best possible position. Once he is lying down (on a soft surface such as grass or carpet), gently roll him over onto one side and over to the other as you say "Roll over!" This is a trick best taught to a puppy, because rolling an adult Rottie can be a physically demanding task. Be sure to reward your dog when he complies with your instruction, increasing your enthusiasm as be begins to roll more of his body on his own. With repetition, he will soon be rolling over with just a verbal cue.

With its many applications, dog training can be a fun and practical undertaking for either the serious trainer interested in participating in obedience or a novice to the pastime. No matter how much time you wish to spend working with your dog, time spent training is time invested in learning how to communicate with your pet. And the better your communication, the better your relationship with your Rottie will be!

83

Chapter 7

In the Doghouse

Proactive training is the best way to prevent your Rottweiler from developing any problem behaviors, but what if you've adopted an older dog who came to you with some unpleasant behaviors already established? Whatever the circumstances, you must address a problem behavior as soon as possible. Putting off dealing with any issue will only make it more difficult. By learning the best ways to deal with the situation, you can help even a dog once thought of as hopeless to finally reach his full potential.

ou may discover that you do not possess the skills necessary to correct the problem by yourself. If this is the case, don't hesitate to seek the help of a professional. Your veterinarian or local animal shelter should be able to suggest a dog trainer or animal behaviorist in your area who specializes in working with more challenging canines. Numerous books and videos also are available to help owners address less intense problems.

Barking

Excessive barking can be a big problem. Not only is it unpleasant for the dog owners themselves, but it is annoying to anyone else within earshot of the noisy pets, too. If your Rottweiler barks too loudly or too often, you may even be faced with a visit from your local police department or costly fines. So if a problem is presenting itself now, the best way to deal with the matter is promptly.

Behavior Modification Technique

When addressing the problem of barking, the first thing you must do is to determine the reason for your Rottie's barking. Many dogs only bark excessively when in a certain environment. Perhaps your dog only barks when he is left in your backyard or when he sees someone walking by your home. The answer may be as simple as not leaving him alone outside or limiting his window access indoors, but avoiding other barking-prone situations (when you are at work, for instance) may be an impossibility. If the problem time is a routine part of your schedule, a more active approach is necessary.

When my breeder told me the best way to teach a dog not to bark, I laughed out loud. I'd asked her advice for solving this problem with my own dogs, who tended to bark most

If your dog barks excessively when left in the backyard, don't leave him alone outside.

when visitors arrived at my home. She was sitting on my kitchen floor with them as she yelled to me (the only way to be heard at that moment), "Have you taught them to bark?" I thought she was kidding; she wasn't. You see, before you can teach a dog not to bark, you must first teach him to bark on command. Sounds easy, doesn't it? Well, it mostly is, but there is a difference between a dog who barks when he wants and a dog who barks when you want him to.

The easiest way to make most dogs bark is by making a noise, such as a knock on a door. By accompanying this noise with the bark (or speak) command, your dog begins to associate the act of barking with the word of your choice. After some practice, making the noise will no longer be necessary. Be sure to praise your Rottie for complying, and then wait for him to stop. As soon as he does (and in the beginning, this may be for only a brief moment), reward him with an edible treat as you firmly say "Enough." Through this training exercise, you teach him that barking is okay, but he must stop when you tell him to. This ensures that he will continue to alert you to any suspicious sounds around your home but that you retain control of the duration of the barking.

If you are not home when your dog's barking is an issue, you may want to consider employing the care of a pet sitter or doggy daycare, both

of which can keep him company and care for his needs.

Biting

Two types of biting occur: playful biting and aggressive biting. In the first situation, your Rottie may grab at your hand with his teeth while you are playing together. He may growl while doing so, but the overall tone is nonthreatening. Many owners find playful biting acceptable, because they perceive no threat from the gesture. Unfortunately, your tolerance of the behavior can inadvertently lead your dog to a more serious, escalated form of nipping, which can hurt others. For this reason, never tolerate any form of biting.

> *Play biting, or nipping, is a nonaggressive form of biting that must nevertheless be dealt with.*

Aggressive biting may fall somewhere within a spectrum of those dogs who act, possessively over food, to those who snap at certain people they do not like, to dogs who outright challenge their owners for a top-ranking position in the family. When they are successful in gaining dominance in one of these areas, most dogs will continue to seek control over other situations as well.

Behavior Modification Technique

Sometimes, all it takes to discourage your dog from play biting is a simple squeal to let him know he has hurt you. (Even if he hasn't actually hurt you, it is best if he thinks he has!) When puppies play together, squealing is a common way to express their dissatisfaction with being nipped. If this doesn't seem to do the trick, you may need to offer a firm "No!" when your dog places his teeth on your body. Remember, even if he is just acting playfully, he must learn that touching you with his teeth is unacceptable.

If your dog begins growling when you or others go near his food dish, don't wait for him to bite before you address the situation. Remove the food, and when it's time to eat again, offer his kibble by hand instead. Again, if he growls, end the meal then and there. Never hit or otherwise punish your dog physically for growling or biting. Remember, violence begets violence; your dog won't understand why it's okay for you to hurt him, but it's not okay for him to hurt you. Your Rottie must understand that you are in charge and that he can trust you not to harm him. You want your dog to respect you, not fear you.

This strategy can be applied to any item over which your dog behaves aggressively, including toys, bones, and special treats. If he behaves aggressively over any of these items, take it away for the time being. When you reintroduce the item, praise your dog for acting appropriately, and even if you leave him alone with the item once again, go back repeatedly to touch it or take it back from him temporarily. Teaching the *drop it* command can also be very helpful when dealing with this kind of problem.

If your dog acts aggressively for what appears to be no reason, help must be sought right away. Talk with your veterinarian, who may want to examine your dog to make sure a physical problem isn't causing the aggressive biting. Remember, you are the responsible party in this situation. If your dog bites another person or animal, you could face steep fines, a lawsuit, and even jail time. You may even be forced to have your Rottweiler euthanized.

Chewing

Chewing can be a particularly frustrating behavior. Given the opportunity, many puppies chew, and nothing is inherently wrong with this. On the contrary, chewing can be a healthy pastime, because it can ease the pain of teething. There's a right way and a wrong

way to indulge this behavior, however. The right way is by providing your Rottie with appropriate items for chewing. The wrong way is to tolerate his ruining other's belongings.

Behavior Modification Technique

One of the most basic ways to teach a dog not to chew indiscriminately is to take unsuitable items away from him. This one step can be extremely effective, but you must be consistent. You may think that allowing your Rottie to enjoy an item that you no longer have any use for is harmless, but even if your dog hasn't yet touched your old pair of slippers, giving him one as a toy will only

The Expert Knows

Aggression

Aggression is considered a true behavioral emergency. Although you may think that your dog would never hurt you or your other family members, even a dog who acts aggressive only with strangers is a ticking time bomb and needs immediate and intensive training. If your dog displays any signs of aggression, including growling, baring his teeth, or biting, get professional help immediately.

confuse him as to which items are acceptable for him to play with and which aren't. Safe, chewable toys meant for a dog your Rottweiler's age and size are the only things he should be given for chewing.

Keeping any tempting items off the floor or out of places where your dog can reach them helps keep your belongings safe. When these kinds of efforts fail, though, your best plan of attack is redirection. When your dog begins chewing anything he shouldn't, simply take the item away and offer him one of his own toys instead. If he accepts the replacement, praise him lavishly. If he doesn't, continue to redirect him (to either the same or a different toy) each time he approaches the inappropriate item in question. Whatever you do, refrain from punishing him for what he has already done. He cannot unchew your new sneakers, but you can take steps to prevent the same fate from happening to your other shoes.

You might be wondering what to do when the item your dog has set his sights on is too big to be taken away from him, like furniture, for example. You shouldn't be expected to completely rearrange your home to prevent your Rottie from reducing your dining room table to firewood. In this situation, you need a safe deterrent, like a bitter apple spray. Products like this have a bitter or otherwise unsavory taste, so your dog won't continue to chew anything that has been sprayed with them. Providing a replacement chew toy will still be helpful in this situation, as well. After all, it is not the chewing you want to discourage, but rather your dog's choice of items to chew.

Digging

For someone who has never dealt with it, the problem of digging may seem like a minor inconvenience. If your dog is making your backyard look more like a gopher sanctuary than a site for a barbecue, though, you know how frustrating this problem can be.

If your Rottie chews on things that he shouldn't, redirect his attention to toys that he can chew.

Finding A Behaviorist

Unlike a trainer, whose work focuses primarily on teaching a dog obedience-related commands, an animal behaviorist observes, interprets, and modifies animal behavior— most often once a serious problem has already arisen. A trainer may be able to help you correct mild problem behaviors, but for more intense problems, a behaviorist is often the best person for the job.

Behaviorists are commonly called into the picture when an animal suffers from a phobia, aggression, or another behavioral disorder. Sometimes a dog and his owner struggle with more than one of these problems, making the advice of this professional even more valuable. But where can you find such a person?

Like trainers, animal behaviorists do not currently need to be licensed to work in this very specialized field, so careful selection is a must. Although a certification process does exist, currently, only a limited number of individuals are certified. You can find a directory of them at www.animalbehavior.org. You can also ask your veterinarian, trainer, or local Rottweiler rescue organization to recommend a behaviorist.

Above all else, you should feel comfortable with the person you choose, but a few other important criteria should factor into your decision as well. Your behaviorist should possess a certain level of education and experience in dealing with animals, particularly large-breed dogs. She should also have dog training knowledge and experience. A degree of some form in psychology or zoology is a definite advantage. Ask for references, and be sure to follow up on them. References from former clients are good, but recommendations from veterinarians and humane societies are even better.

Behavior Modification Technique

To change this behavior, owners must first under-stand why dogs dig. Digging is a very basic instinctual behavior for most dogs, but some circumstances can increase a particular dog's tendency to tear up the ground around him.

Many Rottweilers dig out of boredom. Left alone in a fenced yard with no company, they resort to this destructive method of escaping their dull environment. Perhaps your Rottie is trying to join the dogs he sees walk by the fence each day with their owners, or maybe he has picked up on the scent of a female in the area who has gone into heat. Having your dog sterilized can often help with the latter issue, and getting him out for walks of his own every day is a good idea on all levels. A well-exercised dog will rest more when left alone and will usually amuse himself in less mischievous ways. While on the subject of entertainment, providing your dog with lots of toys can also avert him from decimating your lawn and flowers.

If it is particularly hot or sunny in your yard, your Rottie may be digging to literally carve out a cool place of his own. To eliminate the need for this, always provide him with a comfortable spot to rest out of the sun—and never forget to make fresh water available to him at all times.

Some dogs also dig for simple pleasure. If this is the case for your Rottweiler, consider allowing him to dig in a smaller area that you have specifically designated for this activity. By giving him a place where you not only tolerate but even encourage his digging, you just might save your flower bed and your sanity. Like a child in a sandbox, your dog may likely

thrive when given the chance to repeatedly bury and rescue his beloved bones and toys. If he ventures beyond the realm of this area, simply redirect him to his own space.

Jumping Up

One of the worst things you can do for a friend whose dog jumps up on you is what I did for many years. Trying to be understanding of the pet, I'd instantly reassure him by saying "Oh, that's okay!" What I was actually doing, though, was negating the efforts of my friends who were desperately trying to teach their dogs how to behave properly. I have never minded having a dog jump on me, but the next visitor may. Larger breeds can even hurt someone if not taught to restrain their enthusiasm.

This brings me to the very reason most dogs jump on people—because they want to greet them and because they are happy to see them. You don't have to remove your Rottie from the room whenever company arrives to prevent him from jumping all over your friends, though. You simply need to teach your dog that excitement is fine, but jumping is not. Like so many

If your Rottie enjoys digging up your yard, try giving him his own area in which to dig.

other areas of training, this one requires a lot of practice. An especially good friend may even be able to help you with this. (Just be sure to choose someone your dog really likes, too.)

Behavior Modification Technique

To teach your Rottie not to jump up, ask a friend to repeatedly enter your home so that you and your dog can practice the proper way to greet guests. (Your dog should be able to successfully perform the *sit* command before this time.) When your friend knocks or rings the bell, instruct your dog to sit and wait for him to comply before opening the door. If your dog remains sitting as the visitor enters, allow her to give your Rottie some attention, being careful not to overdo it, of course, as this may encourage him to stand or jump. If he does either of these, stop the attention at once. Ideally, both you and your friend should completely ignore him, backing away if he jumps up. Don't speak to him other than to tell him to sit once more.

You may need to practice the visitor scenario many times before your dog shows progress. Be patient, but don't stop working on this. Of course, when you are expecting someone whom you know either doesn't like or is afraid of dogs, be considerate of her feelings by placing your dog in his crate or in another room before she arrives.

Finding The Lost Dog

If you lose your pet, here are the first five things you should do:

1. Rally your family and friends and go looking. This is especially important if you realize soon that your pet is missing.
2. Call your veterinarian. If your dog is wearing a rabies tag on his collar, the tag number often can be traced to your veterinarian, who can then help reunite you with your lost pet.
3. Call every animal shelter or humane organization in your area. Visit the most likely shelters in person, because you know your pet better than anyone else. Keep checking daily!
4. Check with neighbors and put up signs around your neighborhood (or the area where your pet was last seen). Include a photo or description of your pet, your phone number, and how long your pet has been missing.
5. Call your local newspaper and place a lost pet ad. Also, check the newspaper daily for found pet ads. Often, newspapers print found ads for free.

(Courtesy of the AAHA Healthypet.com)

House Soiling

House soiling (inappropriate elimination) can be one of the most frustrating of all problem behaviors, but fortunately, it can be corrected. The most important thing to remember is that punishment is almost always ineffective in reversing the situation. You must also never strike your Rottweiler, because this only makes him fearful of you—hardly an ideal foundation for remedial training.

If your Rottie's problem behavior is too much for you to handle, consult an animal behaviorist for help.

Behavior Modification Technique

The first step in correcting the problem of house soiling is to schedule a vet visit to rule out a physical cause for the problem. Decreased bladder or bowel control is a symptom of many illnesses, so you must make sure that your dog isn't suffering from one of these issues before creating a plan of action. Only after you have done this can you assume that the problem is behavioral in nature.

Next, you should consider whether your dog's problem falls within the category of submissive urination or excitable wetting. Each of these situations demands a distinctly different approach from true house soiling. If your dog appears to be experiencing a loss of bladder control primarily when he is in the presence of a more dominant individual (this may be a human being or another dog), the culprit is likely submissive urination. If the wetting happens most often when you or other household members arrive home, the problem may be due to overexcitement. In either case, the first step should be to refrain from offering your dog attention at these moments when he is most prone to incontinence. Because both these reactions are involuntary, manipulating the situations will prove more successful than trying to change your dog's reaction to them.

Once you have determined that the problem is indeed house soiling, you must then commit to a new housetraining routine for your pet. A full-grown Rottweiler should be able to go at least four hours between eliminating, but if your dog is typically soiling your carpets after only two or three hours, begin taking him to his potty spot before this smaller length of time passes. You must be consistent and tenacious. Don't return inside your home until your Rottie has eliminated. Once he does, reward him immediately with a heartfelt "Good boy," and consider offering an edible reward in addition to this verbal reinforcement.

Other ways to increase your Rottweiler's chances for success include adjusting his diet during this time so that he is not consuming anything that may alter his elimination schedule. Foods that cause diarrhea, for example, can curb housetraining success, as can foods that cause constipation. For this reason, limit edible rewards to just one or two pieces of your dog's kibble. Also, during this remedial training period, remove your dog's water dish an hour or two before heading to bed each night. Some owners even find it helpful to only offer water with meals until some level of housetraining success is attained.

The one thing that will never solve the problem is punishment. Many rescued dogs were simply never properly housetrained as puppies. When given the opportunity to learn appropriate elimination techniques in a positive environment, these Rotties may become reliable very quickly. Other dogs who might have been abused

SENIOR DOG TIP

Old Dog, New Tricks

People frequently assume that older dogs are incapable of learning. This is not only unfortunate, but it is also untrue. Certainly, training will take a little longer for an older dog who has had time to become more set in his ways, but this is why consistency and persistence are a must.

previously, however, will be held back even more intensely by being punished for their more gradual mastery.

When your Rottweiler is in the proverbial doghouse, all household members can feel like they are stuck there with him. Nothing is fun about having your favorite belongings chewed into oblivion or cleaning urine from your bedroom carpet for the fourteenth morning in a row. Success, on the other hand, can also be catching. Once your dog is on the road to moving beyond his mistakes, you will both feel a sense of pride in your accomplishments. A dog likes hearing nothing more than heartfelt praise from his owner—and you will enjoy nothing more than giving it.

Chapter 8

Stepping Out

Half the fun of sharing your life with a Rottweiler is sharing your fondness for the breed with others. For you, this may be as simple as chatting with those who stop you during walks to ask about your dog, or it may mean participating in more organized activities, such as showing or obedience trials. Whatever your preferences, one thing is certain—if you delight in stepping out with your dog, the two of you can enjoy numerous pastimes together.

Travel and Vacationing

Traveling with a Rottweiler can be a bit more challenging than with more portable breeds, but it isn't nearly as difficult as many people might imagine. When properly planned, a joint vacation can be considerably more fun for both you and your dog than leaving him at home. Unlike your human traveling companions, your Rottie won't even care about where you are going; he just wants to accompany you.

No matter what your mode of transportation, avoid feeding your dog immediately before embarking on any trip. This helps reduce his chance of suffering from motion sickness during the ride. Do make sure to provide him with an opportunity to relieve himself immediately before leaving and again as soon as you reach your destination.

Traveling by Air

In recent years, most airlines have begun welcoming smaller pets into the cabins of the planes, but unfortunately, this courtesy has not been extended to larger breeds, because their crates cannot fit under the seats. Although airlines take many precautions to ensure the safety of dogs traveling in the cargo area, all owners should be aware of a few things before opting for air travel.

The first thing a dog owner should do when planning a trip by plane is to contact the airline. Any questions you may have should be addressed

SENIOR DOG TIP

The Senior Jet-Setter

Perhaps you think your older Rottie might be better off resting his weary bones at home with a pet sitter while you're visiting your Aunt Matilda, but if he has traveled with you in the past, chances are he'd be happier tagging along again. Being left at home may even be more traumatizing for him than any inconvenience he may experience along the way—as long as adjustments are made to make him as comfortable as possible.

When it comes to the older Rottweiler, his best traveling friend is a well-prepared owner. As soon as you know you will be traveling, schedule a checkup with your dog's veterinarian to ensure that he is indeed up to the excursion. Ask whether your dog will need any special preventive treatments or health certificates specific to your destination. If your dog won't be accompanying you, home may indeed the best place for him. For an older dog, the comforts of this familiar setting are preferable to placing him in a boarding kennel or even leaving him at a friend's home. Asking that same friend to pet sit (or hiring a professional) is preferable in this case.

before booking your flight. Because each airline has different rules and regulations, ask for a complete list of these, and allow some extra time to follow up on the requirements. If your dog needs clearances or vaccinations from your veterinarian, for example, it may take longer than you expected to obtain necessary booster shots or just get in for an initial appointment.

Whenever possible, book a direct flight. To make your trip even smoother, try to book your own seat as close to the front of the plane as you can, so you are one of the first people off the plane when it is time to retrieve your pet. You should also expect to pay an additional charge (classified as excess baggage) for the space that your dog will occupy on the plane.

Additionally, the timing of your vacation also matters when planning a flight. Because no temperature-control system is present in the cargo compartment of the plane, it is imperative that you do not travel during extreme weather.

If you are unsure whether your Rottie is a good candidate for air travel, ask your veterinarian. If flying is not a practical option, don't assume you

Allowing your Rottie to ride loose in the passenger seat is a safety hazard for both of you; instead, safely restrain him in the backseat.

must cancel your trip. It may take longer to drive to your destination, but the added peace of mind of knowing that your precious pet is safe is worth even more than the money you'll save on your ticket.

Traveling by Car

Bringing your Rottweiler along on a roadtrip may seem like adding an instant alarm system, but I urge you not to ever leave your Rottie (or any animal) unattended in your vehicle. The potential for disaster—on several levels—is just too great. The heat inside a closed vehicle can reach lethal temperatures in just a few minutes. This is the case in either the middle of summer or in colder weather if you leave the heater running. Leaving the windows open exposes your pet to the alternate risks of running away or being stolen.

Whenever you travel with your dog, his safety must be your top priority. For this same reason, you also should never allow your dog to ride in the front passenger seat; he will be considerably safer in a crate or secured with a canine seatbelt restraint in the backseat.

When traveling by car, schedule regular breaks for elimination and exercise. Also, use this time to refill all water containers. You should hold off on meals until you will be stationary for at least a few hours, but don't forget to hydrate your Rottie frequently during the trip.

Accommodations

Just a decade ago, the idea of finding a hotel that allowed pets was a virtual impossibility. If you were lucky enough to know of such a place, it was likely less than a four-star establishment, to say the least. Fortunately, the hospitality industry has made great strides in recent years by going that extra mile to accommodate their

Rottweilers

Pack His Bags

For many dog owners, the biggest challenge when it comes to packing is knowing when to say when. Pack too little, and you might overlook something important, but bring too much, and you might not have room for your Rottweiler. So how do you determine which items warrant a spot on the list? When packing for my own dogs, I ask myself the following: Do they use this item every day, or would they need it in an emergency? If the answer to either of these questions is yes, it goes along with us. What your Rottie needs while on the road will depend on your individual circumstances, but here is a partial list of what to pack for most roaming Rottweilers:

- an up-to-date photograph in case your dog ever becomes lost
- brush and comb
- crate and blanket or padded insert
- dog license, identification tag (firmly attached to your Rottie's collar), and proof of current vaccinations
- first-aid kit and any necessary medications (including preventive treatments)
- food (for when you reach your destination) and a full water container (for the ride)
- food and water bowls
- leash and collar
- name and number of veterinary hospitals and emergency clinics in the area where you will be staying
- plastic bags and baby wipes
- towel
- toys

guests—people just like you and me who, as it happens, are also dog lovers.

Petswelcome.com, a website that lists a variety of dog-friendly lodging, is an excellent resource for dog owners planning to travel with their pets. In addition to providing travelers with a directory of pet-friendly hotels and motels across the country, the site also offers information on campgrounds, beaches, and even long-term apartments that allow animals.

Sports

Participating in canine sports is a great way to help your Rottie stay mentally and physically fit. You don't have to sign your dog up for every organized activity available to him, but ask yourself if he could benefit from trying one or two. You'll both have fun while strengthening your bond.

Agility

If your Rottie has a penchant for playtime, agility may be a fun activity the two of you can share. This sport requires speed and dexterity, and competitions offer dogs a chance to show off their physical prowess. Resembling an equestrian jumping competition, the setting for agility consists of a variety of colorful jumps, vaulted walks, seesaws, A-frames, and tunnels. Handlers lead their dogs through the course by running alongside them and offering either verbal commands or hand signals (or both) as the dogs navigate these obstacles.

Agility can be as fun for spectators as it is for participants, and the sport regularly draws impressive crowds. Developed in England in the 1970s, it was first recognized by the AKC in 1994. Unlike the requirements for conformation, a dog need not be purebred to compete in agility, and entrants may also be neutered. The one more stringent requirement, however, is a minimum age of 12 months for all canine participants.

Agility requires speed and dexterity.

FAMILY-FRIENDLY TIP

Turning Travel Into Child's Play

Here are a few tips that can make traveling with your whole family a little less stressful for everyone:

1. *Both children and pets need constructive distractions while traveling.* If there is one thing you cannot bring too many of, it's toys—specifically items that allow your kids and your Rottie to entertain themselves.
2. *Everyone must buckle up.* Both children and animals should always be safely restrained whenever riding in the car.
3. *All arms and legs (and heads) should remain inside the ride at all times.* Never allow either your child or your dog to lean out a window while riding.
4. *Never leave children or animals unattended inside a vehicle—ever.* When left alone in a vehicle, both kids and pets are vulnerable to numerous dangers, including heatstroke or frostbite.
5. *Plan ahead.* Write down all the things you will need well in advance of the trip, and use this as a checklist before leaving.

Titles that can be earned in agility include Novice Agility Dog (NAD), Open Agility Dog (OAD), Agility Dog Excellent (ADX), and Master Agility Excellent (MAX). Not everyone who participates pursues all these levels, however, or competes in every competition. Other organizations that hold agility trials include the United States Dog Agility Association (USDAA), the North American Dog Agility Council (NADAC), and the Agility Association of Canada (AAC). Your local Rottweiler club may also sponsor events.

The best thing about agility is that it is something you can do with your Rottie right in your own backyard. You need not ever enter a formal competition to participate, although it might be a lot of fun!

Obedience

Just as some dogs seem destined for conformation or agility, some are amazingly well suited to obedience training. You may notice this when training your dog at home, or this may be your goal from the beginning. All breeds (and mixed breeds) are welcome to participate in AKC obedience trials.

Unlike the sport of agility, which focuses on a dog's physical abilities and allows considerable owner interaction, obedience requires more discipline than athleticism; it is truly a test of how well your dog can do on his own. Among the commands your Rottweiler will be required to perform at the basic level of competitive obedience are heeling (both on and off his leash), sitting and staying for several minutes at a time, and also standing and staying for similarly fixed time periods. Certainly, owners are involved in every aspect of training (and this is no small task), and they are allowed to issue the commands, but you won't find these owners cheering until the day is done.

Dogs begin competing in the Companion Dog (CD) class and then move on to the Companion Dog Excellent (CDX) class, and Utility Dog (UD) class. Ultimately, your Rottweiler has the potential to earn the highest titles—Obedience Trial Champion (OTCh) and Utility Dog Excellent (UDX). Both are considered very prestigious accomplishments that are neither easily nor quickly achieved.

Showing

What image springs to mind when you think of a show dog? A long-haired lapdog in need of constant grooming

Dogs who participate in conformation shows are judged against their breed standard.

and pampering? Of course, more delicate dogs like this are part of numerous conformation shows, but don't disregard the hardier breeds. Many Rottweilers have excellent show potential. They can strut their stuff just as well as the fancier breeds that most people first associate with showing. In several ways, Rotties are even better suited to the activity, because they don't tire as easily as smaller dogs.

You may think your pet Rottie has what it takes to become an AKC champion, but it is vital to understand that, while the Rottweiler can be an ideal show dog, only those dogs who most closely match the breed standard even have a shot of attaining a title in this activity. These dogs usually fetch higher prices than those deemed pet quality by their breeders. So if showing is something you think you might be interested in doing, ask about this before selecting your dog. A show dog should always first be a beloved pet, but unfortunately, most pets fall short of conformation standards. A shortcoming that you might not even notice may be glaringly obvious to a seasoned AKC judge.

The best way to learn about showing is to attend an event in your area. Contact your local Rottweiler club

for information on the nearest upcoming specialty shows, events featuring just the Rottweiler breed. Usually, multi-breed shows (in which the Rottweiler is shown as part of the Working Group) are more common, though, and will therefore provide a quicker opportunity for you to attend an event as a spectator. Points (ranging from one to five) are issued for each win. Dogs who have accumulated a total of 15 points are considered champions. These dogs have earned the right to use the title Champion (abbreviated Ch.) before their names.

While attending a show, visit with the Rottweiler owners and handlers once they have finished in the ring. These experienced Rottie fanciers are usually more than happy to talk to newcomers about their favorite topic—their dogs—once their dogs have had their turn, of course. Ask many questions, and be sure to listen carefully to find out if showing is in fact the activity for you.

Because conformation events began as a means of evaluating breeding stock, show dogs must not be neutered until after they have finished with this activity. No age limitations exist; a Rottweiler may be shown before he is even a year old and for as long as the owner likes. Although the dog must be old enough to understand proper behavior expected in the ring (a show dog must know how to heel, for instance), younger dogs generally fare better in competition than do older ones. There have been a few exceptions to this unwritten rule, however.

Games

Somewhere between participating in organized activities and getting out for a walk with your Rottweiler lies another fun way of providing your dog with exercise—games. Whether you

prefer playing traditional games such as ball and flying disk, or you expose your dog to lesser known canine games such as tetherball, the object is the same: getting your dog moving around and excited over the activity.

Many dogs enjoy playing hide and seek with their owners, but if you try this, make sure that your dog is always the seeker. You should never teach your dog to run away or hide from you. Teaching him to seek you out, on the other hand, can be an excellent means of reinforcing the *come* command.

You can also invent your own games, tailoring them to your dog's individual personality. Do your Rottie's ears perk up whenever you turn on the radio? Maybe he'd delight in bopping around to the music. If he's especially smart, you might even be able to teach him to play a modified version of musical chairs—or at least have some fun trying.

Does your dog enjoy classic dog games, like fetch? Use this to your advantage, and teach him the game of picking up his own toys. (Yes, this really can be done!) Another fun variation of fetch is playing it in the water. Rotties love to swim, so this is a very natural transition for them. The choices are as limitless as your

imagination. Above all else, remember how much fun your Rottweiler brings to your life, and never stop trying to think of new ways to bring joy to his.

Try to see this entire chapter as a starting point for finding fun ways to spend time with your beloved pet. Perhaps your dog is more of a homebody and prefers running around in the backyard to performing in front of an audience. Or maybe he likes hiking and exploring with you on the weekends more than trekking around the same neighborhood every evening. No matter what activities you choose to enjoy with your Rottweiler, one thing is certain—he will be happier for every moment you spend with him.

Your Rottie may enjoy noncompetitive games, such as flying disk.

Resources
Associations and Organizations

Breed Clubs

American Kennel Club (AKC)
5580 Centerview Drive
Raleigh, NC 27606
Telephone: (919) 233-9767
Fax: (919) 233-3627
E-mail: info@akc.org
www.akc.org

Canadian Kennel Club (CKC)
89 Skyway Avenue, Suite 100
Etobicoke, Ontario M9W 6R4
Telephone: (416) 675-5511
Fax: (416) 675-6506
E-mail: information@ckc.ca
www.ckc.ca

Federation Cynologique Internationale (FCI)
Secretariat General de la FCI
Place Albert 1er, 13
B – 6530 Thuin
Belqique
www.fci.be

The Kennel Club
1 Clarges Street
London
W1J 8AB
Telephone: 0870 606 6750
Fax: 0207 518 1058
www.the-kennel-club.org.uk

United Kennel Club (UKC)
100 E. Kilgore Road
Kalamazoo, MI 49002-5584
Telephone: (269) 343-9020
Fax: (269) 343-7037
E-mail: pbickell@ukcdogs.com
www.ukcdogs.com

Pet Sitters

National Association of Professional Pet Sitters
15000 Commerce Parkway, Suite C
Mt. Laurel, New Jersey 08054
Telephone: (856) 439-0324
Fax: (856) 439-0525
E-mail: napps@ahint.com
www.petsitters.org

Pet Sitters International
201 East King Street
King, NC 27021-9161
Telephone: (336) 983-9222
Fax: (336) 983-5266
E-mail: info@petsit.com
www.petsit.com

Rescue Organizations and Animal Welfare Groups

American Humane Association (AHA)
63 Inverness Drive East
Englewood, CO 80112
Telephone: (303) 792-9900
Fax: 792-5333
www.americanhumane.org

American Society for the Prevention of Cruelty to Animals (ASPCA)
424 E. 92nd Street
New York, NY 10128-6804
Telephone: (212) 876-7700
www.aspca.org

Royal Society for the Prevention of Cruelty to Animals (RSPCA)
Telephone: 0870 3335 999
Fax: 0870 7530 284
www.rspca.org.uk

Rottweilers

The Humane Society of the United States (HSUS)
2100 L Street, NW
Washington DC 20037
Telephone: (202) 452-1100
www.hsus.org

Sports
International Agility Link (IAL)
Global Administrator: Steve Drinkwater
E-mail: yunde@powerup.au
www.agilityclick.com/~ial

North American Flyball Association
www.flyball.org
1400 West Devon Avenue #512
Chicago, IL 6066
800-318-6312

World Canine Freestyle Organization
P.O. Box 350122
Brooklyn, NY 11235-2525
Telephone: (718) 332-8336
www.worldcaninefreestyle.org

Therapy
Delta Society
875 124th Ave NE, Suite 101
Bellevue, WA 98005
Telephone: (425) 226-7357
Fax: (425) 235-1076
E-mail: info@deltasociety.org
www.deltasociety.org

Therapy Dogs Incorporated
PO Box 5868
Cheyenne, WY 82003
Telephone: (877) 843-7364
E-mail: therdog@sisna.com
www.therapydogs.com

Therapy Dogs International (TDI)
88 Bartley Road
Flanders, NJ 07836
Telephone: (973) 252-9800
Fax: (973) 252-7171
E-mail: tdi@gti.net
www.tdi-dog.org

Training
Association of Pet Dog Trainers (APDT)
150 Executive Center Drive Box 35
Greenville, SC 29615
Telephone: (800) PET-DOGS
Fax: (864) 331-0767
E-mail: information@apdt.com
www.apdt.com

National Association of Dog Obedience Instructors (NADOI)
PMB 369
729 Grapevine Hwy.
Hurst, TX 76054-2085
www.nadoi.org

Veterinary and Health Resources
American Animal Hospital Association (AAHA)
P.O. Box 150899
Denver, CO 80215-0899
Telephone: (303) 986-2800
Fax: (303) 986-1700
E-mail: info@aahanet.org
www.aahanet.org/index.cfm

American Holistic Veterinary Medical Association (AHVMA)
2218 Old Emmorton Road
Bel Air, MD 21015
Telephone: (410) 569-0795
Fax: (410) 569-2346
E-mail: office@ahvma.org
www.ahvma.org

Resources

American Veterinary Medical Association (AVMA)
1931 North Meacham Road – Suite 100
Schaumburg, IL 60173
Telephone: (847) 925-8070
Fax: (847) 925-1329
E-mail: avmainfo@avma.org
www.avma.org

ASPCA Animal Poison Control Center
1717 South Philo Road, Suite 36
Urbana, IL 61802
Telephone: (888) 426-4435
www.aspca.org

British Veterinary Association (BVA)
7 Mansfield Street
London
W1G 9NQ
Telephone: 020 7636 6541
Fax: 020 7436 2970
E-mail: bvahq@bva.co.uk
www.bva.co.uk

Publications
Books
Anderson, Teoti. *The Super Simple Guide to Housetraining*. Neptune City: TFH Publications, 2004.

Libby, Tracy. *The Rottweiler*. Neptune City: TFH Publications, 2006.

Morgan, Diane. *Good Dogkeeping*. Neptune City: TFH Publications, 2005.

Magazines
AKC *Family Dog*
American Kennel Club
260 Madison Avenue
New York, NY 10016
Telephone: (800) 490-5675
E-mail: familydog@akc.org
www.akc.org/pubs/familydog

AKC *Gazette*
American Kennel Club
260 Madison Avenue
New York, NY 10016
Telephone: (800) 533-7323
E-mail: gazette@akc.org
www.akc.org/pubs/gazette

Dog & Kennel
Pet Publishing, Inc.
7-L Dundas Circle
Greensboro, NC 27407
Telephone: (336) 292-4272
Fax: (336) 292-4272
E-mail: info@petpublishing.com
www.dogandkennel.com

Dog Fancy
Subscription Department
P.O. Box 53264
Boulder, CO 80322-3264
Telephone: (800) 365-4421
E-mail: barkback@dogfancy.com
www.dogfancy.com

Dogs Monthly
Ascot House
High Street, Ascot,
Berkshire SL5 7JG
United Kingdom
Telephone: 0870 730 8433
Fax: 0870 730 8431
E-mail: admin@rtc-associates.freeserve.co.uk
www.corsini.co.uk/dogsmonthly

Index

111

Index

Dedication

To my loving husband Scot and our amazing son Alec. I love you both
more than words can say.

Acknowledgments

I would like to thank the following people for taking the time to speak with me about their
experiences with Rottweilers:

Dany Canino, AKC Judge
Ginger Hanson, Ginger's Rottie Rescue
Pam Grant, President, American Rottweiler Club
Juan J. Greigo, Redondo Rottweilers
Judy Marion, Founder and President, NoVa Rottweiler Rescue League, Inc.
Michele Mauldin, Owner
Lew Olson, American Rottweiler Club Disaster Committee Member for Hurricane Katrina
Diane Sacripanti, Founder and Treasurer, North Carolina Rottweiler Rescue

About the Author

Tammy Gagne is a freelance writer who
specializes in the health and behavior of
companion animals. She is a regular contributor
to several national pet care magazines and has
owned purebred dogs for more than 25 years. In
addition to being an avid dog lover, she is also an
experienced aviculturist and writes a bimonthly
column that appears in *Bird Times* magazine.
She resides in northern New England with her
husband, son, dogs, and parrots.

Photo Credits

Front cover photo courtesy of Gordana Sermek (Shutterstock).
Photos on pages 14, 18, 24, 28, 30, 34, 45, 46, 56, 61, and 88
courtesy of Pet Profiles; Lara Stern.
All other photos courtesy of Isabelle Francais and T.F.H. archives.